A
CHINDIT'S
CHRONICLE

A
CHINDIT'S
CHRONICLE

Bill Towill.

Authors Choice Press
San Jose New York Lincoln Shanghai

A Chindit's Chronicle

Authors Choice Press
an imprint of iUniverse.com, Inc.

For information address:
iUniverse.com, Inc.
5220 S 16th, Ste. 200
Lincoln, NE 68512
www.iuniverse.com

Originally published by Quacks Booklet Printers

ISBN: 0-595-15832-3

Printed in the United States of America

TABLE OF CONTENTS.

ORDER OF THE DAY

(Issued to Columns as they crossed the Chindwin,
13th to 17th February, 1942)

Today we stand on the threshold of battle. The time of preparation is over, and we are moving on the enemy to prove ourselves and our methods. At this moment we stand beside the soldiers of the United Nations in the front line trenches throughout the world. It is always a minority that occupies the front line. It is a still smaller minority that accepts with a good heart tasks like this that we have chosen to carry out. We need not, therefore, as we go forward into the conflict, suspect ourselves of selfish or interested motives. We have all had the opportunity of withdrawing and we are here because we have chosen to be here; that is, we have chosen to bear the burden and heat of the day. Men who make this choice are above the average in courage. We need therefore have no fear for the staunchness and guts of our comrades.

The motive which has led each and all of us to devote ourselves to what lies ahead cannot conceivably have been a bad motive. Comfort and security are not sacrificed voluntarily for the sake of others by ill-disposed people. Our motive, therefore, may be taken to be the desire to serve our day and generation in the way that seems nearest to our hand. The battle is not always to the strong nor the race to the swift. Victory in war cannot be counted upon, but what can be counted upon is that we shall go forward determined to do what we can to bring this war to the end which we believe best for our friends and comrades in arms, without boastfulness or forgetting our duty, resolved to do the right so far as we can see the right.

Our aim is to make possible a government of the world in which all men can live at peace and with equal opportunity of service.

Finally, knowing the vanity of man's effort and the confusion of his purpose, let us pray that God may accept our services and direct our endeavours, so that when we shall have done all we shall see the fruit of our labours and be satisfied.

O.C. WINGATE, Commander,
77th Indian Infantry Brigade

NOTE. This was the Order of the Day for "Operation Longcloth", the first Wingate operation.

PREFACE.

At one time or another, many of us will have toyed with the idea of writing up some aspect of our wartime experiences, only to dismiss it almost immediately. After all, who on earth would want to read what we have to say, might it not be misconstrued as unacceptable pretensions to literary skill and perhaps, most important of all, why should we indulge in "line-shooting" when much better men with far more to say, have kept silent. I fear that for better or worse, these and any similar misgivings have, so far as I'm concerned, been resolved by others and I've found myself wrestling inexpertly with my little word processor, wishing that I could type and desperately struggling to meet a deadline.

On 1st. October, 1990 my old battalion the 3rd/9th Gurkha Rifles will celebrate the 50th anniversary of its re-raising and from its commandant in India came a request to supply them with "a few pages" about the battalion's involvement in the Chindit operation in 1944 - a task to be fulfilled, not reluctantly but with gratitude and pleasure as we look back on those heady days of long ago. The request was made to one of our senior officers, who has deputed me to carry out the job. As the account gradually evolved I became convinced that to make it reasonably intelligible to those who have no real knowledge of all that happened so long ago, or of the old Indian Army, and hopefully to make it more interesting, I would have to digress. The extent and nature of those digressions are apparent from the text. Parts of the account are largely from personal recollections but I hope they will not prove to be unduly ego-centric.

For the details, obviously not retained in memory - and many of those retained are as sharp as they ever were - I have had to rely on other books and records, including our regimental history, not always strictly accurate in some respects, some old maps which I still possess, some contemporaneous notes by Alec Harper, very kindly unearthed and sent to me by Alan Watson - to whom I am much indebted - and also a visit to the Imperial War Museum in London. I should have liked much more time for research, but have been beaten by the deadline and perhaps most of all by my almost complete lack of typing skills, which has made the compilation of each page a very considerable effort. With all its defects and shortcomings, I present it as a simple and affectionate tribute to those wonderful little men with whom I served so long ago.

There comes to mind the oft quoted and moving tribute to the Gurkhas penned by Professor Sir Ralph Turner, M.C., who was adjutant of the 2nd/3rd Gurkha Rifles in World War 1 in the preface to his great "Dictionary of the Nepali Language" - the poetic beauty of his words strike a chord in my own heart and memory and will, I venture to say, do the same for anyone else who has suffered hardship and danger by their side:-

> "As I write these words, my thoughts return to you, who were my comrades, the stubborn and indomitable peasants of Nepal. Once more I see you in your bivouacs or about your fires, on forced marches or in the trenches, now shivering with wet or cold, now scorched by a pitiless and burning sun. Uncomplaining you endure hunger and thirst and wounds; and at the last your unwavering lines disappear into the smoke and wrath of battle."

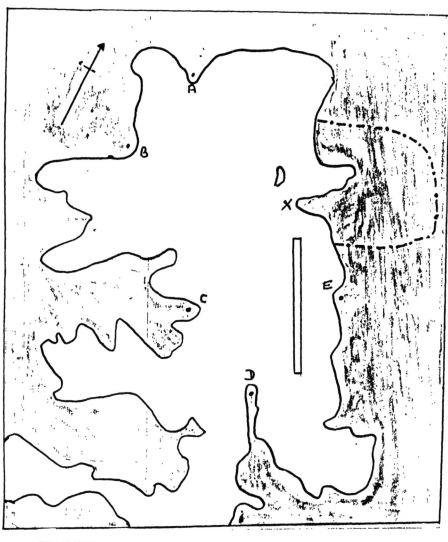

BROADWAY.

A copy of a contemporaneous sketch map in my notebook. My notes show that small standing patrols, of a rifle section or rifle or Bren group, were maintained at the following six points, the approximate magnetic bearings from point X being - A 300; B 270; C 195; D 172; E 145 and R 173. The radar set was located at point R, having been moved from its previous location, which was a clearing to the east of our perimeter. The perimeter wire is shown by a line of dots and dashes and the airstrip was to the south west as shown by long rectangle. The map is to the scale of approximately 250 yards to the inch.

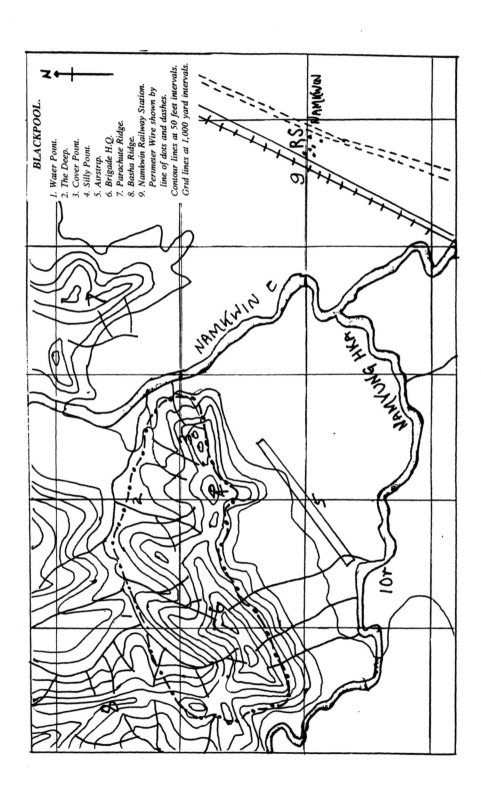

BLACKPOOL.

1. Water Point.
2. The Deep.
3. Cover Point.
4. Silly Point.
5. Airstrip.
6. Brigade H.Q.
7. Parachute Ridge.
8. Basha Ridge.
9. Namkwin Railway Station.
Perimeter Wire shown by
line of dots and dashes.
Contour lines at 50 feet intervals.
Grid lines at 1,000 yard intervals.

NAMKWIN C

NAMYUNG HKA

NAMKWIN

9 R.S.

A CHINDIT'S CHRONICLE.

by Bill Towill, ex 3rd/9th Gurkha Rifles.

PROLOGUE.

The late afternoon sunshine glinted on the wings and fuselage of a great armada of aircraft which crowded the small military airstrip at Lalaghat, about 70 miles west of Imphal in Assam. At one end of the runway some 80 large Waco troop carrying gliders were drawn up, two abreast, in a long queue and ahead of them were laid out, with careful precision, the nylon tow ropes, which within a couple of hours would be hooked up to the Dakota aircraft, now assembled at the far end and around the edge of the strip, to speed us eastwards well behind the Japanese lines into occupied Burma. As soldiers of the 14th Army, not without reason dubbed "The Forgotten Army" and used to having to make do with outdated equipment and a chronic shortage of military supplies, we gazed around us with awe and incredulity at this impressive panoply of hardware, provided by courtesy of Uncle Sam - or, to be more precise, the 1st Air Commando of the U.S.A.A.F. Their genial and very businesslike commander Col. Phil Cochran and his deputy, Col. Alison, both of them famous fighter aces, had greatly impressed us by their obvious ability and desire to give us maximum support. Amongst their glider pilots was the renowned film actor, Jackie Coogan.

It was Sunday, 5th March 1944 a couple of days before the night of the full moon, selected with special care so that the landings, codenamed "Operation Thursday" which would occupy about five days, would be able to take maximum advantage of the moonlight. Although we couldn't possibly know this, it also happened to be exactly three months and one day before the greatest sea borne invasion in history was to hit the coastline of Normandy, at dawn on the 6th June, under the codename "Overlord", which was to lead eventually to the end of the war in Europe. It was therefore little short of miraculous that our commander, Major General Orde Wingate, was able, in face of such competition, to secure these facilities for his division, the 3rd Indian Division, otherwise known as Special Force and later to become famous as "The Chindits". The name derived from our divisional sign, which depicted the Chinthe, a mythical winged lion-like creature, whose image sejant,carved in stone, was to be found ubiquitously guarding the temples of Burma.

THE BACKDROP.

Early in 1942, in a matter of weeks, the Japanese had evicted the British from Malaya and Burma, gaining in the process an aura of invincibility. For many months the enemies had faced each other, on the central front, across the general line of the River Chindwin in a position of stalemate, with little activity, apart from clashes between patrols, on either side. To the west, in the coastal area known as the Arakan, an attack, in which our battalion played a part, was launched southward early in 1943 in an attempt to wrest the port of Akyab from the Japs, but this had foundered, with heavy losses, against their massive defences at Donbaik, resulting in a position of stalemate on this front as well. At Donbaik, the Japanese occupied a system of deep bunkers, carefully sited so that they could each bring covering fire to bear on their neighbours. The tactics employed by our forces had been classic 1914-18 - an intense artillery bombardment followed by a direct frontal assault by massed infantry - and had resulted in classic casualties. The bombardment though spectacular was ineffective and left the bunkers and their occupants largely intact.

On one occasion, by a sad mischance and repeating what had happened in the Great War, the barrage had lifted fifteen minutes before our men had reached the objective, giving the defenders ample time to emerge from the depths of their bunkers and man their machine guns. By great dash and courage many of our troops managed even to get on top of the bunkers, only to come under devastating machine gun and mortar fire from adjoining enemy strongpoints. On 18th February, the 2nd/1st Punjabis, commanded by Lt. Col. A.W.Lowther, D.S.O. lost about half their number, within the space of half an hour in such an attack. Shortly afterwards when our brigadier fell ill and was evacuated, he took command of our brigade and told us of this desolating experience. Other similar attacks with British troops including the Royal Welch Fusiliers, Royal Scots, Durham Light Infantry and the Lincolns met the same fate and supporting tanks were knocked out at close range by anti-tank fire.

On the northern front, where the famous Ledo Road was being constructed to provide a route for supplies between India and China, the American Lieutenant General Stilwell ("Vinegar Joe") was operating south of the road in the Hukawng Valley, with two Chinese divisions under his command and a small American force, colourfully known as "Merrill's Marauders", though, as yet, little marauding had been done on that front either.

Between February and May 1943, Wingate then a brigadier commanding 77 Brigade, had led his brigade on foot on a guerilla expedition behind the Japanese lines (known as "Operation Longcloth") and had been supplied by air. A copy of his inspiring Order of the Day issued for that operation is included at the front of this book. His force had suffered heavy casualties and endured appalling hardships but had successfully demon- strated that the Japanese were by no means as invincible as they appeared to be. He became convinced that a large force, landed behind the Japs and supplied by air, could decisively swing the course of the war in this theatre in our favour. He committed these ideas to a brilliant report on "Operation Longcloth", which contained sixteen appendices detailing every aspect of his new strategy, and ensured that this was sent to London to be read by the Prime Minister, Mr. Winston Churchill. He also had no inhibitions about arranging that his audacious exploits became front page news. The Prime Minister read the report, observed the news items and, unhappy about the course of the war in Burma, took the extremely unusual course of summoning this comparatively junior officer (Wingate was still only a brigadier) to 10, Downing Street, London. They met there over dinner on 4th August 1943 where Wingate discoursed at length and so eloquently on his concept of what he called "Long Range Penetration Groups" that Churchill determined to take him on the morrow aboard the Queen Mary on his long planned voyage to Quebec.

With them went the Chiefs of Staff and though much of the time was spent planning details of Operation Overlord, a day was set aside for the campaign in South East Asia, when Wingate addressed them at great length and all were taken by his imaginative ideas, his supreme confidence in his ability to make them succeed and the forceful eloquence and cogency with which he expounded them. In Quebec, they conferred with the Americans and Wingate made a great impression on General H.H.Arnold, the Commander of the U.S.A.A.F. from whom he received a promise of the air support, which his plans required.   The performance of that promise, or at least an earnest of it, was there displayed before our eyes at Lalaghat that Sunday afternoon, though as lowly figures in the drama, we then had no idea of what had gone before.

The other side of the coin was that Wingate's turbulent and most abrasive character, his direct access to the Prime Minister and Chiefs of Staff and the conversion of all these vast resources to the support of his plans, were unlikely to win him friends in the thicket of senior commanders which, had he followed convention, he ought to have traversed to get to the top. Anything that could properly be done to put down this upstart and frustrate his "harebrained" plans was likely to be done.   This factor also strongly coloured many of the appreciations which were subsequently made of the operation and of Wingate personally. But for the fact that he enjoyed the patronage and protection of General Sir Archibald Wavell, the Commander in Chief, India, who recognised the talents of this exceptionally difficult man, his plans might well have been frustrated.

THE SCENE IS SET.

Limited though our knowledge might have been, we could not but be aware, as we gazed around the airstrip, that this was a moment of history, a moment to savour, to confide to the innermost recesses of our memory, so that those of us who outlived this day and the battles and searing hardships which lay ahead and came safe home, would always be able to say with pride, "I was there! " It was to be the biggest operation of its kind so far launched during the War, and was to involve locating five infantry brigades, almost the strength of two normal infantry divisions, well behind the enemy lines and supplying them by air.

One of the brigades, the 16th Brigade under the command of Brigadier Bernard Fergusson, who had been one of Wingate's column commanders in the previous year's operation, and later, as Lord Ballantrae was to be Governor General of New Zealand, had already marched beyond the Chindwin and well behind the Japanese lines. The 77th Brigade, of which we were a part, commanded by Brigadier Michael ("Mad Mike") Calvert, also one of Wingate's previous column commanders and his closest confidant, was to spearhead the airborne landings, to be followed by 111th Brigade (Brig. W.D.A. Lentaigne); 3rd(West African) Brigade (Brig. A.H. Gilmore); 14th Brigade (Brig. T. Brodie) and Morris Force an offshoot of 111th Brigade commanded by Lt.Col.(later Brig.) J.R. ("Jumbo") Morris, 4th/9th Gurkha Rifles. Yet another brigade, 23rd Brigade (Brig. L.E.C.M. Perowne) originally part of Special Force was removed to take part in the fierce battle around Kohima and Imphal.

The objectives of this great airborne invasion were to block the flow of supplies and reinforcements northwards to the Japanese 18th Division, who were facing General "Vinegar Joe" Stilwell and his combined Chinese and American forces in the Hukawng Valley along the Ledo Road to China; to inflict maximum confusion loss and damage on the Japanese and to create a situation which might induce the Chinese Army to cross the Salween and enter the conflict in Burma.

We had but recently joined the Chindits. On 27th January 1944 to our considerable surprise, we were mysteriously ordered to leave our old comrades in the 4th Indian Infantry Brigade of 26th Indian Division in the Arakan. Only after we had left them at Fenua, did we learn that we had been transferred to 77th Indian Infantry Brigade (commanded by Mike Calvert) in Special Force whom we then joined at Monacherra in the United Provinces for a few weeks of hectic training before finding ourselves alongside the gliders at Lalaghat. I have no doubt that our transfer to Special Force came about because we had been hand picked by Wingate.

On the 17th May 1943 our battalion relieved the 1/17th Dogras at Taung Bazaar on the east of the Mayu Range in the Arakan. A few days after they arrived, a villager came in before dawn to report that there was a party of Japs - he estimated about 50 men and two officers - in the village about a thousand yards from "C" company's position on the west bank of the Kalapanzin river. Major F.G. ("Jimmy") Blaker set off with "C" company to investigate and caught the enemy resting in a nullah. Few of them had time to put on their equipment and some even fled naked. Their only sentry was on top of a small hill and was armed with a light machine-gun and he opened fire on the leading platoon. Havildar Danbir Kharki crawled up to him, making use of some intervening dead ground, threw his hat to one side to distract him, and followed this up with a grenade, which finished him off. He then turned the machine-gun on to the enemy, who fled pursued by Jimmy and his men. After a chase of nearly two miles, they killed 16 Japs and captured 3 wounded Japs, including the first Jap officer to be taken in the Arakan, for the loss of two of our men killed - one by a swordstroke through the head - and a few lightly wounded.

For a Japanese, capture was the ultimate disgrace and their wounded routinely killed themselves with a grenade rather than suffer capture, so the capture of a Japanese officer was of great significance. On a front where there was little encouraging news this brisk little action received wide publicity and we even had to surrender one of our best riflemen to act as a personal orderly for our divisional commander. I'm sure Wingate heard of this and was able to requisition us for his force and, whilst he was at it, took our 4th battalion as well since they, so to speak, were out of the same stable. Jimmy was awarded a well deserved Military Cross and later was to cap this with the Victoria Cross - sadly posthumously.

We joined Special Force at an awkward time when the efforts of all were directed towards perfecting the details of last minute planning and consequently did not receive the attention we might otherwise have received, but our first visit from the 'General, which occurred at Hailakandi, was notable. The normal formalities might well have been expected - the whole of the battalion on parade, drawn up in revue order, called to attention by the colonel and then to present arms as the buglers sounded the measured and majestic notes of "The General Salute", to introduce the General's inspection of the parade. The reality could not have been more at variance with this scenario and I cannot do better than to quote verbatim the vivid account which Scott Leathart, then our adjutant, has retrieved from his diary:-

"We have seen very little of the senior officers who are to command us in the coming operations, but this morning I received, as Adjutant, a signal informing us that General Wingate will be visiting us tomorrow at 1000 hrs. I was ordered to construct a 30 ft square sandpit to be marked by 1 ft grid squares by strings across both ways. I chose a spot for the pit below a gentle curving mound so that officers could sit above the pit and see clearly what the General intended to show us. Much digging in the hot sun by a fatigue party resulted in a very neat job such as Gurkhas are adept at doing. The much depleted QM store had, by good fortune,a large roll of somewhat loosely-wound string and with this we were able to make the grid lines. This evening, when all was finished, the Jemedar Adjutant and I were able to look upon this handywork with some pride.

"Five minutes before the appointed hour this morning, we were all seated above the pit in the warm sunshine confidant that the General would have no cause for complaint about the execution of his orders. After a considerable wait, a small cloud of dust appeared at the far end of the airstrip and from it appeared two ponies galloping "ventre a terre" in our direction. They bore down upon us and it seemed that they must flash past. But all of a sudden they reined up, the ponies rearing up just like in a cowboy film, and came trotting towards us. We could then see that the leading pony, which from its blotchy appearance seemed basically to be white but here and there dyed khaki, carried the General. He sported a beard, in contravention of King's Regulations, and on his head was an old battered Wolseley solar topi. The rest of his uniform, bush shirt and slacks, was far from clean and exceedingly creased. On the other pony was the ADC immaculately dressed.

"The General leapt from his mount, handing the reins to his ADC, and strode over to Noel George whose salute he acknowledged without taking his cane from his hand. He then turned and gazed at us with his piercing blue eyes. Having taken us all in, he ordered us to sit down in the sandpit while he stood where we had expected to sit, and gave us a short pep talk. Despite my disappointment, even anger, with his peremptory disregard of our work on the pit in accordance with his orders, I found myself greatly impressed with him and what he had to say. He exuded confidence in what he and we were about to do and I got the impression that he would always somehow know what the Japs would do in any situation brought about by his tactics, and he would thus be able to press home any advantage. Having wished us luck and assured us that we were in for a hard, but rewarding, time, he leapt on to the pony and disappeared in a cloud of the same dust which had heralded his arrival, leaving us astonished but somehow more confident."

On the other fronts things were also beginning to move. In the Arakan, which we had just left, 5th and 7th Indian Divisions had, on New Year's Eve 1943, attacked south on either side of the Mayu Range, with 81st West African Division out on their left flank in the Kaladan Valley. Against stern opposition they had managed to reach the road running from west to east across their front and connecting Maungdaw on the coast with Buthidaung to the east via the famous Tunnels. They had been held up by the Japanese fortress position at Razabil, where the north to south road intersected the east to west road near Maungdaw, but had succeeded, by the end of January, in capturing sufficient of the fortress area to neutralise the enemy position, though the fortress itself still held out. Though this represented considerable progress, it was still 13 miles short of the position at Hyparabin, which our brigade had reached the previous March, before being forced to fall back.

Meanwhile, the Japanese 55th Division decided to implement a plan formulated months earlier and, on the night of 3rd February 1944, splitting into three separate forces, Kubo to the north, Doi to the south and Tanahashi in the centre, they swung out in a wide right flanking movement, avoiding the conflict along the Maungdaw to Buthidaung road. They moved so skilfully and swiftly that they achieved complete surprise and, in the darkness, the administrative base (soon to become famous as the "Admin Box") of the 7th Indian Division at Sinzweya at the eastern end of the Ngakyedauk Pass (dubbed the "Okedoke Pass") over the Mayu Range, found itself under fierce attack by some 8,000 enemy. Before the night ended 7th Divisional H.Q., some four miles away, was also under attack, and splitting up into small parties, Major General Messervy and his staff fell back on the Admin Box through the enemy infested countryside. Within the next few hours the Japanese had blocked the passes over the Mayu Range thus severing communications between 7th and 5th Divisions and also the supply routes for both divisions. They did not, however, secure the stranglehold they believed they had, because they had reckoned without the RAF and the USAAF and their ability to supply the beleaguered forces by air. The Battle of the Admin Box was to become famous, but it was only part of the action by the two divisions and of the 26th Indian Division (our old Division) and 36th Division, both of which moved south to aid the two forward divisions. It was not until 23rd February, after fierce fighting, that the British-Indian forces could claim victory in this theatre.

In point of fact, this hard fought action had been intended by the Japanese to be a diversionary attack aimed at drawing away our forces from the northern front, where they were to follow up with their main thrust, codenamed "Operation U". For this they employed three divisions, the 33rd was to approach Imphal from the south, the 15th, starting ten days later, was to attack Imphal from the north whilst the 31st, swinging further north, was to capture Kohima, astride the road from the railhead at Dimapur to Imphal and so to exert a stranglehold on the only supply route to our forces in the Imphal plain and to the south of Imphal on the Tiddim road along the line of the Chindwin. It was on 7th March, only two days after the commencement of our own operation, that elements of the 33rd Division brought pressure to bear on our forces around Kennedy Peak on the Tiddim front and on the approaches to Imphal from the south.

On the 17th March the Japanese crossed the Chindwin in strength and their Operation "U" was in its first phase. General Slim decided that the decisive battle would be fought on the Imphal plain and to concentrate his forces there, which meant that our two forward divisions, spread out along the line of the Chindwin, had to be withdrawn to Imphal. Under his orders the 17th Indian Division covering the most southerly part of the front at Tiddim fell back via Bishenpur, whilst to the north of them the 20th Indian Division fell back to Palel. Further north the heroic stand of our men at the village of Kohima along the vital road link from Dimapur to Imphal was destined to capture the imagination of all. The name is probably the first to come to mind when anyone thinks of the war in that area and most could quote the poignant words inscribed on our war memorial there - "When you go home, tell them of us and say - 'For your tomorrow we gave our today'". It was against this unfolding background that our own operation was launched and those of us engaged in it confidently believe that it played a most significant and effective part in undermining the Japanese offensive.

THE SUNDAY THAT WAS THURSDAY.

Lt. Col. Noel George, the C.O. of the 3rd/9th Gurkha Rifles, with myself as his Intelligence Officer and a section of our men as an advance party of the battalion were due to take off in one of the leading gliders. We were in the port tow of, I think the fifth pair of gliders to leave the ground. The starboard glider in our pair had on board Peter Fleming, the famous author (accoutred as a Lt. Col. in The Grenadier Guards) who was also the husband of the actress Celia Johnson, later to bring many of us great delight with her superb performances. With him was our attached R.E. officer, Lt. Leigh-Mallory, who was both the son of the famous mountaineer, who had died only a few years previously in an abortive attempt to conquer Mt. Everest, and also the nephew of Air Marshal Sir Trafford Leigh-Mallory, the commander of the Allied Expeditionary Air Force for Operation Overlord. To even things up a bit, they also had a couple of mules on board! Loading a recalcitrant mule on to a glider or Dakota is not a task to be undertaken for the fun of it, but these contrary animals were essential to our plans. They carried our 3" mortars, our Vickers medium machine guns, our spare ammunition and equipment and most importantly of all, our radio sets which were our sole means of contact with base. Despite their evil temper and waywardness, we grew to respect, even to love them. For mile after weary mile I was later to trudge along the jungle paths of Burma, behind a particularly fine specimen, known as "Taxi", who carried our radio set.

As we waited for sundown and "H" hour, we were exhilarated by the prospect of what lay ahead. Although we affected a fashionable veneer of cynicism and would not display our innermost thoughts, below this facade our true feelings ran deep. We were young, most of us very young, and extremely patriotic. We were convinced of the justice and righteousness of our cause and that, one day, right would prevail and that victory would be ours. We wanted to do our part in achieving that victory, whatever the cost. Though we had been with Special Force for only a few weeks, we had caught some of the enthusiasm and zeal of our most unusual commander and could see that his imaginative plans had every prospect of success and felt proud and privileged to be part of them. No one who has ever served with the Gurkha soldier has anything but the greatest respect and admiration for his splendid qualities - his courage, his toughness, his unquestioning loyalty, his discipline, and his unfailing and unquenchable cheerfulness even under conditions of great hardship and danger. We were going out into the unknown - we knew not what lay ahead but could count on having to contend, at the very least, with extreme hardship and danger - but it was a great comfort to be going out into the unknown with such men, not as strangers but as tried and trusted comrades in arms, bound together by the strong family ties of the battalion. If we had even to pass through the valley of the shadow of death, then we could not do so in better company.

Some of us with strong religious beliefs - and no doubt others who would not openly admit to such beliefs - silently committed ourselves to God's keeping. We had checked all our weapons and equipment time and again. There was little to do but wait. Sitting under the shade of a tree, I drew from my breast pocket a small book called "Daily Light" which had been given to me by my mother and contained random passages from the Bible, set out as morning and evening readings for each day of the year. I turned to the pages for the evening of 5th March and the morning of 6th March. Some of the words I read seemed surprisingly apposite and I drew comfort from them - "The angel of the Lord encampeth round about them that fear him, and delivereth them"...."The Lord your God ... went in the way before you, to search you out a place to pitch your tents in... to show you by what way ye should go"...."As an eagle stirreth up her nest, fluttereth over her young, spreadeth abroad her wings, taketh them, beareth them on her wings so the Lord alone did lead him.." ..."With us is the Lord our God to help us and to fight our battles."

Just before "H" hour an act of high drama occurred - so high, in fact, as to put the whole of the operation in the balance and for several minutes it was uncertain as to whether the entire operation would be aborted. We were due to land in two jungle clearings codenamed "Broadway" and " Piccadilly", about 260 miles away to the east and in the crook of the mighty Irrawaddy River, where at Bhamo, having flowed south, it suddenly changes to a generally westerly course in a wide "S" loop before reverting at Katha to its generally southerly course towards Mandalay 150 miles to the south. In that crook a sizeable tributary, the Kaukkwe Chaung, running north to south enters the right bank of the Irrawaddy. About 10 miles north of that confluence and to the east of the Kaukkwe was Piccadilly and 25 miles further north was Broadway. Another force, including our own 4th battalion, was to be landed on the following night at "Chowringhee" further to the south.

For security reasons, Wingate had imposed a strict embargo against overflying these sensitive areas. At 11am on the 5th March, Capt Charles Russhon of the U.S. Army Photo Reconnaissance Unit, with "H" hour less than seven hours away took off in a Mitchell B25 Bomber piloted by Col. Smith, for a final look at the landing sites. They were acting in flagrant breach of Wingate's orders, but carrying out what they regarded as a reasonable precaution, with permission from Col.Cochrane which they'd obtained after pressing him repeatedly. Broadway was clear and so was Chowringhee, but what they found and photographed at Piccadilly sent them back to their laboratory at Hailikandi at top speed to process the pictures and send them by fighter plane the short distance to Lalaghat where they were seen by Cochrane and Alison, who immediately ran over to Wingate with them. To their great dismay and consternation, they saw that Piccadilly had been blocked by hundreds of great teak logs. Landing there would have resulted in almost total carnage, but a more important question arose. Had security been compromised; were the Japs even now waiting at Broadway to annihilate the invaders as they landed and ought the operation to be called off?

There were frantic consultations involving General Slim, 14th Army Commander, Air Marshal Sir John Baldwin, Wingate and Calvert whilst other senior generals who had come from G.H.Q. to see us off stood by. Some of them probably would not have been unduly distressed had Wingate's plans come a cropper! Standing by our gliders, we saw the top brass conferring but without fully realising what was at stake, though their anxiety was apparent. Despite the risks and uncertainties it was decided that the operation should go forward with all the landings of our force diverted to Broadway and at 6.08 pm, only a few minutes later than planned, the first pair of gliders took off.

We wheeled our own glider forward as each pair ahead of us took off. Then our own turn came, we clambered aboard, were hooked up and lumbering and grumbling down the runway, steadily gathered speed in a cacophony of sound until suddenly, all was silent and we realised we were airborne and gaining height rapidly. I was sitting just behind the pilot and, looking over his shoulder, soon realised that all was not well. He was wrestling with the controls and trying to trim the glider whilst the glider on our starboard kept swinging in towards us dangerously. Suddenly he reached up and punched at the lever above his head, the tow line fell away and the glow of the tug's exhausts receded into the distance whilst we banked steeply and in total silence, apart from the sound of the wind rushing past the fuselage, headed back along the flight path we had been following.

Below us, in the brilliant moonlight I could see the open paddy fields, with the paddy bunds lying directly across our path, rushing up towards us at 70 miles per hour. I saw the pilot put his feet up on the dashboard and he then yelled out - "Hang on ... there's going to be a bump!". Spreadeagling my hands above my head, I hung on to two convenient struts - we had no seatbelts - lifted my feet in the air, indicated to my men to do likewise and waited in this ungainly posture for the crash, expecting any moment to end up with my backside ploughing the fields!. Then we hit the ground. In a rending, drumming, tearing,grinding, crashing tumult of sound we bucketed and bounced our way over the paddy bunds hanging on for dear life as we were violently jolted around and the glider filled with choking dust until after a few seconds which seemed like an eternity, we came to a juddering halt. Apart from being shaken up and a little bruised most of us had suffered no harm, though one man at the rear of the glider sustained a broken arm.

The pilot had done a remarkably good job. The paddy bunds (substantial mud walls built up two feet or more from the general level of the paddy fields) presented a formidable and extremely dangerous obstacle to a glider landing at high speed. Had we come in at the wrong angle and hit one of the paddy bunds head on, or crashed it too hard with our tail, we could easily have been flipped over on to our back, with some broken necks as a result. A few red Verey lights fired into the air and, before long, transport picked us up and we were in line again, standing alongside another glider and hoping for better luck.

Before our turn came, the lengthy silence from Broadway was broken at 2.30am by two words, in clear, coming faintly through the static and repeated three times - "Soya Link, Soya Link, Soya Link!" Nothing else - just this pre-arranged code to stop all flying. Nine tows already in the air were recalled and eight returned to Lalaghat, whilst the ninth went on to Broadway. The success signal - "Pork Sausage" - never came and there was no other message to relieve the gloom and despair keenly felt by Wingate and his staff as they were left to speculate on what had gone wrong. Then at 6.30am, to everyone's immense relief, came the message "Pork Sausage", calling for flying to be resumed that night. By 10am radio conditions had improved sufficiently to enable Calvert to speak to Wingate; 30 men had been killed and 28 injured, not by enemy action but in the glider landings, some of them in the crashing gliders, others struck by incoming gliders whilst working to build the airstrip. Of the 61 gliders despatched only 34 had arrived , but there had been sufficient men to prepare a rough airstrip able to receive Dakotas that night. Col. Alison had managed to land with equipment to control the incoming flights and Major Andy Rebori of the USAAF courageously took in a group of Sentinel L5 light planes, flying very low, to bring out the wounded and so initiated a life saving service which we later took almost for granted.

It later transpired that of the 27 gliders which had not reached their destination, 6 landed in enemy territory, one of them close to a Japanese divisional Headquarters near Pinlebu, and the remainder landed in Assam. Those which landed beyond the Chindwin, were spread out over a wide area and served to confuse the Japs as to what was happening. Their passengers often had their own private little battles with the enemy. Even our starboard tow, no longer endangered by the presence of our glider, did not reach Broadway, but crashed on a sandbank in the Chindwin, leaving its occupants to swim the fast flowing waters, if they could, to get home.

Later experience showed that the Waco gliders could carry not more than 3,500 pounds. This limit had, in fact, been grossly exceeded with loads of 4,500 pounds plus extra items smuggled aboard by some of the troops. This made the gliders extremely difficult to fly. They climbed very slowly and reluctantly; they failed to respond to the controls and, after release by their tug, they entered into a steep dive accelerating to a speed greatly in excess of their proper landing speed. Only by employing all their physical strength and skills were the pilots able to avert disaster, and some of them were just not able to make it. As they crossed the mountain range along the Burmese border they encountered bumpy conditions, stressing the gliders and tow aircraft even further. Tow ropes slackened and then abruptly snapped taut like bowstrings, putting the aircraft in great jeopardy. One glider, as it lost height on the far side of the mountains, found itself accelerating so fast in the mist and cloud, which obscured the tug, that it came up alongside the tug and only by outstanding airmanship was the pilot able to correct this, take up the slack in the tow rope and resume correct station behind the tug.

BROADWAY ESTABLISHED.

In the few hours available to them, the small force at Broadway, with the aid of a miniature bulldozer landed fortuitously enough by the very last of the gliders to arrive, had achieved little short of the miraculous in building a rough airstrip which that night received no less than 61 Dakotas and their loads, including our own very small advance party, held over from the previous night. To stand alongside the strip, only a very few brief hours ago no more than a clearing in the jungle, and see the aircraft landing and taking off again, just as if it were a busy civil airport, brought a sense of exultation I shall never forget. Early the next morning, with a handful of other officers, I sat on the ground in a semicircle in front of Wingate, who had also made the journey overnight. Always keen to lead from the front, he had insisted on making an appreciation of the situation at first hand. He complimented us on the initial successes, expressed regret at the casualties, adding that you "can't make an omelette without breaking some eggs" and spoke of the struggle that still lay ahead. Though sombre, he radiated a quiet confidence and an almost messianic sense of mission and he had the uncanny, almost hypnotic ability through his clipped speech and magnetic personality to transmit those intense feelings to his audience.

As though to emphasise what he was saying, there came the rattle of small arms fire and the crump and crash of grenades and mortar bombs from a couple of hundred yards behind us.

Turning our heads, we saw a dense column of smoke rising from the top of the jungle canopy at the edge of the clearing. One of the gliders, missing the clearing, had crashed high up into the tree tops, killing its passengers. It had not proved practicable to recover the bodies from the tangled web of twisted metal and timber, so the wreckage had been set on fire. As the flames reached the haversacks and ammunition pouches a macabre firefight ensued, with bullets and shrapnel tearing into bodies which only short hours ago, vibrant and sentient, had, for the last time, rejoiced at the glory of a new dawn and felt sunset's glow.

The conference over, the brigadier took our small party to the other side of the clearing. He was wearing his formal hat with its red band but the chinstrap, instead of languishing on top of the peak of the hat, as is usual, was around his chin to keep the hat securely in place, though there was no wind. Before dealing with other matters, he decided to impart some important jungle lore. He indicated a large creeper hanging down from the trees, which could normally be relied on to carry a supply of potable water and, in a scene reminiscent of Moses striking the rock at Horeb, took a mighty swipe at it with his kukhri, severing it cleanly. But no water flowed. We made a careful mental note of the creeper, with an addendum to sharpen our kukhris first, since a fair amount of slashing might well be necessary before we struck lucky!

Brigadier "Mad Mike" Calvert was of medium height and quietly spoken and his daring, personal courage and bravery were almost legendary and had earned him his soubriquet, as well as a D.S.O. in Operation Longcloth. He was to win a bar to his D.S.O. for his work in the opening stages of Operation Thursday. Three weeks later, flying from Broadway by light plane, Wingate visited his commanders in the field, for what was to be the last time, since, before the night was out, he was to perish in an air crash. He conferred with Calvert and, as he said farewell to his trusted lieutenant, he placed his hand on Calvert's shoulder and said: "Oh, by the way, you have got a bar to your D.S.O. Let it go to your heart and not to your head!" But such an injunction was, in Calvert's case, quite superfluous. In establishing the road and rail block at Henu later on, he was personally to lead a bayonet charge to dislodge the enemy from the top of Pagoda Hill and to engage in the ferocious hand to hand fighting which followed - and I'm sure that not many brigadiers can have had that experience and even fewer would have relished it as he did. Apart from this great reserve of personal courage and fighting spirit, he was a soldier of great skill and imagination, who as Wingate's closest confidant shared many of his ideas and much of his flair. We felt greatly privileged to be in his brigade.

About a hundred yards within the jungle, we came upon a shallow valley, little more than a fold in the ground, at the bottom of which ran a sizeable stream of crystal clear water, which would meet the battalion's needs adequately. We were on the fringe of a mature teak forest - teak had been one of Burma's major revenue earners - many of the trees were massive specimens and their dense canopy high above our heads had the effect of inhibiting the normal proliferation of the undergrowth, which instead of being dense as it so often was in Burma, was comparatively light, with grass about two feet high. There was nothing to disturb the tranquil beauty of this idyllic sylvan setting - there was the babbling brook and the sleepy sound of the chirruping of myriads of cicadas which clustered on the trees and looked at us unafraid with their saucer-like eyes, but we could not help wondering how long this peace would last.

Here we set about laying out the general outline of the defensive position to be occupied by the battalion so that, as they arrived during the next two nights, we would be able to guide them into their allotted positions smoothly and swiftly. It was to form what Wingate termed a "stronghold" - a position so well fortified as to be virtually impregnable against normal attack and a refuge to which the roving columns could return from time to time for rest and replenishment. Expecting a ground attack at any moment, we dug furiously and without let up - I remember digging all night without a break.   The individual foxholes were of a keyhole shape, the long portion roofed in with substantial timbers from the almost inexhaustible supply in the jungle all around us and covered with earth to afford a shelter which would be proof against mortar fire, and with the round part of the keyhole recessed to form a fire step.   As supplies arrived we wired ourselves in with a double wall of triple Danert barbed wire entanglements.

By the time we'd finished we had an almost impregnable fortress comprised of dozens of bunkers covered by an interlocking fire plan, with its western flank along the edge of the jungle overlooking the airstrip.   The strip, lit by paraffin flares, hour after hour throughout the night resounded with the roar of aircraft ceaselessly landing with more men and animals and supplies at the rate of one landing or take off every three minutes.   This truly astonishing flight plan was controlled from a centre set up in one of the crashed gliders.

Once again I am grateful to my old friend, Scott Leathart, for his impressions of his flight into Broadway.   He says:-

"It is odd how litle I recollect of that fateful night.   We were taking part in a very risky enterprise; we might be shot down or career into the mountains in bad weather; we might crash on landing, for putting down on an improvised strip at night must be very hazardous; and we might be engaged by the Japs before we had time to deploy.   Yet we never thought for one moment that any of these calamities would overtake us.   We emplaned full of confidence and good cheer and were airborne without any real apprehension.

"I remember very little about the flight, except that we sat on hard benches along each side of the aircraft, with our bulky packs between our knees,each, no doubt, with his own thoughts becoming blurred and rambling as fitful dozing overcame the initial wakeful anxiety.   As we gained height to cross the mountain range which topped in many places more than 7,000 feet, the clammy heat which we took with us from the ground soon gave way to a dry chill, at first welcome but later such that many of the men unstrapped their blankets and wrapped themselves up.

"After an hour or so, the silver line of the Chindwin River could be seen snaking its way south towards the Irrawaddy.   The drone of the engines changed to a less urgent note and our ears began to pop as we lost height.   Then in the even blackness of the jungle below yellow lights appeared, marking out the landing strip at Broadway.   Slowly we circled, peering through the windows as other planes made their final run in with landing lights ablaze.   It was an astonishing scene; in a jungle clearing - a few days previously nothing more than that - were scores of transport planes, alighting briefly to disgorge their loads of 30 or more men, and roaring off again into the night to let others take their place.   Our turn to land came and we sank swiftly towards the jungle, the engines cutting back and coughing as we bounced along the rough grassy strip.   The door was opened and we jumped out on to Burmese soil.   Guided by the Advance Party, we marched in single file along the edge of the airstrip, the smoky smell of paraffin flares assailing our nostrils and the roar of aircraft in our ears.   Soon the grim evidence of the glider mishaps could be seen in the flickering light; upturned machines, their wings shatttered by the dense growing trees; their flimsy fuselages ripped and torn by the force of their loads breaking free in the headlong rush to destruction; and most poignant of all, the sickly stench of death so quickly generated in the humid heat - a smell which was to accompany us throughout the next few weeks. Once in amongst the trees, we bivouaced as best we could, spending the night in insect plagued discomfort; but at least we were safely on the ground and intelligence reports sugggested that the Japs were unaware of what was happening."

Capt. Guy Hepburn came in with a troop of four 25 pounders from "U" troop of the 160th Field Regiment R.A. and we dug emplacements for his guns along our western flank overlooking the airstrip. A radar post was set up in a clearing to the east, in a rather vulnerable position I thought, but it had to be clear of the jungle to operate effectively. We also had fighter cover in the shape of half a dozen Spitfires, which alternated with a similar number-of Mustangs and we were also joined by Major Andy Rebori and his light plane force of mixed L1 and L5 Sentinel aircraft. His men, I'm sorry to have to admit, provoked some of us to envy. Not for them just half a blanket at the bottom of a foxhole, but before our wondering eyes there appeared most luxurious contraptions known as jungle hammocks, slung between two convenient trees. Constructed of jungle green waterproof material, they incorporated a canopy to protect the occupant from the rain and, below that, mosquito netting, with a zip opening, linked the canopy to the main part of the hammock. If, by our own fairly primitive standards, they might in certain respects have appeared to be pampered, they were, in truth, men of immense resource and courage, who landed their flimsy aircraft in the most improbable and dangerous locations to pick up wounded and bring them back to Broadway, whence Dakotas took them back to hospital.

On Operation Longcloth, the first Wingate operation, everyone knew and accepted that if they sustained a wound which pre-vented them from marching, they would be abandoned in the jungle and left to their own fate - they could not expect the progress of their column to be in any way impeded by having to carry wounded with them. So it was that many men with comparatively slight injuries, which would readily have responded to proper medical treatment, were left in the jungle to die alone and unattended. A few were rescued by friendly villagers, who at the risk of fearsome reprisals by the Japanese, harboured them and nursed them back to health. Many, recognising the inevitability of their fate, speeded the process by a self administered bullet or grenade. This uncivilised attitude to the wounded could not but be a cause of grave concern not just to the survivors, who had suffered the unforgettable pang of leaving their comrades to die, but also to all who later received a report of the operation. Thus it came about that, for Operation Thursday and the ensuing campaign, special arrangements were made to deal with wounded and the sufferings of many of them were alleviated by the mercy missions flown by Major Rebori and his band. The Broadway stronghold with its many sided services was commanded by Colonel Claud Rome, who had a brigade major as his chief staff officer.

CHOWRINGHEE COMPLETES THE FIRST PHASE

Sixty miles to the south of us and on the far side of the Irrawaddy another jungle clearing code-named "Chowringhee" after the name of the main street in Calcutta, had been used on 6th March to land twelve gliders, one of them piloted by Jackie Coogan, carrying 100 men from our 4th battalion commanded by Major Ted Russel together with Major Anderson and Lieuts Craddock, Wilmot, Shipston and Langford but most unfortunately the glider containing a small bulldozer crashed.   Nevertheless, those who had landed succeeded, by dint of Herculean efforts and with hand tools only, in constructing a rough airstrip which was able that same night to receive some Dakotas the first of which was piloted by General Old from Texas, the commander of Air Transport Command. After a quick survey, most of the airborne Dakotas were ordered by radio to return to Lalaghat, but a glider carrying another bulldozer and five other Dakotas with supplies and some American combat engineers were allowed to land.

There followed another night and day of back breaking toil before the strip was ready to receive regular traffic. Waves of Dakotas then came in at twenty minute intervals that night and the next two nights bringing the remainder of the battalion and also the 3rd battalion of the 4th Gurkha Rifles together with the headquarters of 111 Brigade, but with a Japanese air attack imminent, the strip was then abandoned.   The other two battalions in the brigade, the 1st Bn. The Cameronians and the 2nd Bn. The King's Own Royal Regiment had been landed at Broadway, so that Brig. Lentaigne suffered the disadvantage of having his brigade split into two. The landings at Broadway so over-shadowed the initial days of the operation, that the truly remarkable achievements of Ted Russel, his officers and men in opening the airstrip in 24 hours by hand labour alone has never received the recognition it deserved.

The forces which had landed at Chowringhee now split into two. The basic Chindit fighting unit was the column, in effect a half battalion comprising two rifles companies with its own support groups of 3" mortars and Vickers machine guns, headquarters and radio and our 4th battalion was organised as two columns - 49 and 94 Columns, which then began to operate separately from each other as they moved eastwards. The first obstacle to be crossed was the Shweli, a tributary of the Irrawaddy, but a mighty river in its own right, some 350 yards wide. An airdrop of rubber rafts and assault craft was arranged, which enabled 94 Column to cross the river near Wingaba Cliffs, due east of Chowringhee, on the night of 14/15th March and 49 Column to follow the next night. Thereafter, as "Morrisforce", the two columns operated to the east of the Irrawaddy, quite independently of the rest of their brigade, and with considerable success against the Bhamo-Myitkyina road, a main Japanese artery of supply for the North Burma front.

Meanwhile brigade headquarters and 3rd/4th Gurkha Rifles, organised as 30 and 40 Columns, had moved west and faced the even more formidable barrier of the Irrawaddy. At the chosen crossing point, just south of the village of Inywa, a large sandbank about 300 yards wide and a mile long, reduced the width of the stretch of water which they had to cross to 600 yards and also provided a convenient landing ground and dropping zone.

A flare path, comprised of bundles of driftwood, was laid out on the sandbank, and at each stood a man with a match and as they heard the approaching Dakotas, the fires were lit and the parachutes dropped along the runway. Half an hour later, three more Dakotas arrived, each towing a glider on a single tow. All three gliders landed without incident and disgorged all the necessary equipment for the river crossing, though two of the gliders had been badly damaged. Later another Dakota returned trailing a tow rope which engaged a special snatch-up apparatus, that was erected on poles marked by lights, and set up to one side of the undamaged glider. With this mechanism the Dakota lifted the glider straight up into the air in an astonishing technique perfected by our American friends and headed back for Lalaghat. Aboard it were the three glider pilots and four Burma traitor police captured some hours previously and drugged to keep them quiet.

The heavy engines and boats had all to be carried half a mile to the assembly point and by the time the first boats were ready to make the crossing, the night was far spent and there was clearly little prospect of completing the crossing before daylight, with the grave risk of being caught in the midst of the operation by enemy aircraft. As if this were not bad enough, several of the boats engines failed to function properly and at one stage there were only two serviceable boats. These difficulties were then compounded by yet another. The mules refused to cross the river. They went in the water up to their knees, but then turned back. Attempts were made to swim them across, but even after they had got half way, some of them turned around and came back. They tried towing them behind the boats and though some success was achieved with this method, often mules would pull the boat around until it went out of control and would end up where it started.

A request was made for continuous air cover and, shortly after dawn, all were greatly heartened by the arrival of the first flight of Mustangs. But as the hours slipped by, the risk of an enemy ground attack intensified and the brigadier had to make the agonising decision of leaving one column behind if the crossing were not completed by 3pm. Rafts were constructed and two outboard motors mounted on each and this proved more successful in shipping the mules across, but by 3pm only 30 mules had made the journey. Colonel Monteith with 40 Column (half of the 3rd/4th Gurkha Rifles) was left behind with the mules that did not make the crossing with orders to join Morrisforce (4th/9th Gurkha Rifles) who had travelled east. Brigade headquarters and 30 Column (the remainder of the 3rd/4th Gurkhas) completed the crossing as quickly as they could, but with only 30 mules available, instead of the full complement of about 100, much of the heavy equipment had to be jettisoned.

This completed the first phase of the operation. Within a period of six days, in a total of 78 glider and 660 Dakota sorties, 9,052 troops, 1,360 pack animals and 250 tons of supplies had been landed in a brilliantly successful operation for the loss of a total of only 121 men killed or wounded - and all these casualties were exclusively among the glider men. At that time it was an achievement unequalled anywhere in the world. Wingate issued his exultant Order of the Day:-

> "Our first task is fulfilled. We have inflicted a complete surprise on the enemy. All our columns are inserted in the enemy's guts. The time has come to reap the advantages which we have gained.
>
> The enemy will react with varying tactics, but we will reconquer our lost territory in North Burma. Let us thank God for the success he has vouchsafed us and press forward with our sword in the enemy's ribs to expel him from our territory. This is a moment to live in history; it is an enterprise in which every man who takes part may feel proud to say one day, 'I was there'."

ABERDEEN COMPLETES THE FLY-IN.

Two further brigades remained to be landed in Burma - 14th Brigade, with its four British battalions and the 3rd (West African) Brigade with its two remaining battalions of the Nigeria Regiment (one of the Nigerian battalions had already been landed at Broadway) and these were flown in to another airstrip code-named "Aberdeen" constructed by Bernard Fergusson and his men of 16th Brigade, who had marched all the way in. The 6th battalion of the Nigerian Regiment which landed at Broadway had a disastrous experience. Marching away from Broadway towards Aberdeen, where they were to garrison the stronghold, they had, near the railway, run slap into a well prepared ambush laid by Major Wakayuma and his battalion of 146 Regiment from 56 Division, and took a heavy beating and were scattered. Wingate was outraged and furious that this had happened and gave strict instructions that they were to be given no help or succour - if they came to us they were to be turned away. I gathered that he took the view that this could not possibly have happened had strict march discipline been observed. To bump into a party of the enemy was one thing, but to give them sufficient notice of your approach to lay an elaborate ambush was quite another. Although we did not know this, that same enemy battalion was on its way to attack us at Broadway and we were to have the opportunity of settling the score.

Aberdeen   lay about 60 miles almost due west of Broadway, close to the village of Manhton and a few hundred yards east of the Meza river, yet another tributary of the Irrawaddy.   In his book "The Wild Green Earth", Bernard Fergussson tells how,early on the morning of 22nd March, five gliders arrived over Aberdeen, each on a single tow, carrying the equipment required for the construction of the airstrip - bulldozers, jeeps and carryalls as well as American engineers to operate them.   Out of one of the gliders clambered a large, rather portly and flustered pilot, who announced rather surprisingly that he was going to church in future. Apparently, over the mountains the tow rope got wrapped around his front wheel and he promised that if it came off he was going to church in future.   It did come off - and he was looking for a convenient church! His name was Jackie Coogan. Within thirty six hours the strip was ready to receive Dakotas and the two brigades were flown in with all their equipment.   Thereafter it took an increasing share of the traffic that had previously used Broadway.

MUTAGUCHI MISCALCULATES.

One of the most remarkable books on the war in Burma is "Burma - The Longest War" by Louis Allen (published by J.M.Dent), which ought to be purchased by anyone with an interest in the war in the Far East. Mr Allen served during and after the War as a Japanese-speaking intelligence officer and from this great advantage and with access to both public and private archives in London and Tokyo and also from conversations and correspondence with Japanese as well as those on our side of the fence, he has been able to produce a quite unique account as seen from both sides. From his account it is clear that the Japanese gravely underestimated the size of the Chindit invasion. Major General Tazoe, the commander of the Japanese airforce in Burma, had a shrewd idea of how it might develop, and early in March, he flew to Maymyo to speak to General Mutaguchi, the commander of the 15th Army (equivalent to our Army Corps), which comprised the three divisions engaged in the attack on Imphal.

He told him of the various landings, that the road and rail serving the 18th Division had been cut at Mawlu and heavy fighting was in progress. He opined that the landings could soon blossom into a tremendously strong unit in the very heart of the Japanese rear communications. They could cut off Myitkyina and then nothing could prevent Stilwell's road going through to China, which would result in the Japanese forces in China, being brought under great pressure, with possibly attacks even on Japan itself from

China based US planes. Given these implications, he urged that every unit should be hurled against the invaders, even if it meant postponing the Imphal operation. The ebullient Mutaguchi, who considered himself little short of invincible, rejected these arguments. Perhaps they had landed a couple of hundred gliders, but how were they going to supply the men they had dropped?. Whilst they were scuttling around Katha, he would be into Imphal and cut the line to Ledo and they would just wither on the vine. Tazoe argued that his superior just did not understand the transport capacity of the planes. With 300 planes they could shift 1,800 tons a day and if they achieved only 20% capacity, this meant 30,000 tons a month, the equivalent of using 100 trucks a day. Mutaguchi would have none of it, let them do what they liked with their airborne units, they were just "a mouse in a bag", he would cut at their very roots in Ledo, he'd never lost a battle yet, the gods were with him. As Winston Churchill might well have said - "Some mouse! - some bag!"

So concerned was Tazoe that he flew to Rangoon to reason with General Kawabe, the Commander in Chief Burma Area Army and Mutaguchi's superior. Though Kawabe took the landings more seriously, he added that it would be unthinkable to cancel the Imphal operation and perhaps it would be better to leave it to Mutaguchi. Kawabe knew Mutaguchi well and had been his brigade commander in Peking in 1937 and thought highly of his military acumen.

BROADWAY BOMBED.

At Broadway things continued to remain quiet and we steadily improved our defences and looked around for other things to do, apart from the continual patrolling. Prospecting amongst the crashed gliders, I obtained a severed wing and several perspex windows and hauled them back to my patch inside the perimeter. The wing was lashed in an upright position between two trees and on one side I carefully mounted a set of all the one inch maps I possessed, and on the other side the half inch and quarter inch maps and over this melange I nailed the perspex windows. It was then a simple task to mark up with chinagraph pencils, details of enemy dispositions and movements in blue and of our own forces in red as information came in on the daily sitrep from Base, or from other sources, such as our own patrols and columns, as well as the local Kachin tribesmen, who were very friendly and frequently passed information to our Burma Rifles detachment. During lulls in other activities, this proved to be a favourite meeting place for our officers and served two very useful purposes. It kept them informed of current intelligence and also as they pored over the maps, so conveniently displayed, they extended their knowledge of the local geography. My chief concern was that all this information should not be handed to the enemy on a plate, if we were overrun, so I rubbed out any sensitive details after they had been seen by all.

Looking through one of my old notebooks, I came across a remarkable story from one of our men, Rifleman 99690 Nar Bahadur who got lost, though how he contrived to do so is not recorded. As an aside, perhaps I might add that a majority of our men had regimental numbers well up into the 10,000 range - the "das hazar wallahs" - and his lower regimental number signifies that he was a rather more senior soldier and ought to have had more sense. However, I quote his story verbatim, as it appears in my original pencil note:-

"I was on the airstrip fatigue on the night of 12th-13th March. At 0500 hours I attempted to find my way back to the camp but got lost in the jungle. I walked towards the setting moon (probably NW) and the noise of the airplanes was behind me. At 0900 - 1000 hours I was captured by a party of 8 enemy who were coming towards me along a fairly good path in no set formation. They caught me, bound my arms and took me back in the direction from which they had come. They wore Japanese khaki caps with a yellow St. Andrews cross about the size of a rupee piece on the front of the cap. They wore white blouses, something like battledress with white collar patches on which was some black lettering. They wore waist belts with two pouches, one on either side and long puttees. Their boots were in bad condition. They were armed with SMLE pattern rifles only.

"When we reached a large river an hour after my capture, we had already crossed 4 or 5 small streams. This river was about 40 feet wide and waist deep. We reached camp soon after dark, walking along a fairly good path and not crossing any more streams. The camp was about 20 yards from a stream not quite as big as the one we had previously crossed. At the time of our arrival there were only five other men in the camp, but later others came in from patrol to make up a total of about 20 to 25 men. My rifle and everything in my pockets was taken away and my boots exchanged for an old worn out pair. The enemy kept their food in sacks and that night gave me some rice and vegetables and fed me both in the morning and evening of the next day (14th March). They smoked cheroots and cigarettes made from tobacco leaves and gave me a cheroot to smoke. After they had eaten their morning meal at about 0900 hours, patrols left the camp.

"On the night of 14th March two sentries were posted whilst the rest slept. In the early hours of 15th March at about 0300 hours, I undid the ropes tying my hands, took a rifle from the pile and ran away. I heard no alarm. I walked through the jungle more or less in the direction from which I had come. Passing through the big river once again, I saw a lot of fish and shot one with the rifle.On the night of the 15th/16th March I was in the jungle and on the afternoon of the 17th March approached Broadway from the south, found a small stream west of the old brigade HQ area and walked up it until I came to a path, where I turned to the right and came to the airstrip from the NW corner. I've got a sore heel but with new boots and socks could lead a patrol to the enemy camp tomorrow morning 19th March."

As a result of this man's story a patrol left Broadway at 0800 hours on 19th March consisting of two platoons of 82 Column and one section of Gurkhas with Lieut. Jackson ("Jacko"). After a considerable amount of uncertainty and several false starts, Nar Bahadur found and recognised the path he had followed. My note gives the map references of the route followed by the path which eventually led the patrol to three bashas (native huts constructed of bamboo) near the banks of the Namkho Chaung, which must have been the river he referred to. There were the remains of cooking fires which had been extinguished some days previously and also some elephant droppings. On questioning, Nar Bahadur admitted he had seen one elephant with the party and from noises he had heard, thought there had been more some yards away in the jungle. A local who was questioned said that the bashas had been erected the previous year by people who, from his description appeared to be members of the BTA (The Burma Traitor Army, who were a force of dissident Burmese organised by the Japanese).

Some patrols were organised to invest local villages believed to contain dissidents and to question them. My notes record one such patrol to accompany Major Cook of the Burma Intelligence Corps (he was an old Burma hand with many years experience of the country) to the village of Mischo Sakan and to bring back any prisoners he might decide to take. The patrol was to leave the Stronghold at 0800 hours on 13th March and was to comprise 81 Column and, from our battalion, Lieut. M.H.Bates one section each from "A" and "D" Companies, 2 signallers with a 48 set and 2 Gurkhas from the Intelligence section. The men of 81 Column were to "box" the village to prevent any villagers from escaping, and interrogation was to be carried out by Major Cook. The party from our battalion were then to escort Major Cook and any prisoners back to the Stronghold, whilst 81 Column patrolled to the south. Each man was to carry 3 days "K" ration. I'm not sure what happened on this patrol, but similar patrols were successful in capturing known traitors, even some who were recognised as having betrayed to the Japanese some of our men who had been on Operation Longcloth two years previously.

On 13th March about 20 Japanese Zero fighters attacked and strafed and bombed us, wounding a couple of riflemen and damaging the radar and four light aircraft, but otherwise causing little damage. Five Spitfires took off against the raiders, downing four of them for the loss of one Spitfire. On 16th March the attack was repeated by twelve medium bombers with a fighter escort who dropped anti personnel and 500lb. bombs, when two of them were shot down, but three Spitfires were destroyed on the ground.

During one of the air raids, I think it was this one, our second in command Major P.B. ("Schultz") Keilly had an interesting experience. He had taken it upon himself to train some of our men as snipers and was personally illustrating the practice of Jap snipers of strapping themselves high up in the treetops and taking shots at targets down below. He had strapped himself high up in a choice position when the air raid alarm sounded, but believing it to be a false alarm he took no action. When the first stick of bombs came hurtling down with the noise like an express train, he found himself enjoying a grand stand view, which I'm sure he would gladly have surrendered. With trembling fingers he managed to free the strap and descend to the ground just before the aircraft came back on their return run with their second stick of bombs.

On 20th March there was an even heavier air raid, which still left us intact, but more significantly a heavy ground attack was just about to hit us.

THE WHITE CITY ESTABLISHED.

After completing their sterling work of building the airstrip at Broadway, Calvert and the remainder of his brigade, at noon on 8th March marched west to what became known as the "Railway Valley". For a distance of some sixty miles northwards from Mawlu, the road and railway which comprised the main supply route for the Japanese 18th Division facing Stilwell and his forces in the Hukawng Valley, ran side by side through quite a narrow valley, hemmed in on the east by the Gangaw Range, rising in places to 4,500 feet, and on the west by a tangle of hills, which if not so imposing as the Gangaw Range were equally difficult to traverse. A glance at a one inch map of the area will give some idea of the immense difficulty of the terrain. The contour lines crowd into each other and swing back sharply on to myriad black lines converging upon each other, betokening steep slopes intersected by a multitude of steep sided valleys, carrying rivulets and streams which feed into each other until they become substantial water courses. This craggy, jungle covered terrain is traversed only by footpaths - and even they are few and far between.

To ponder a map is one thing, but to plod those tracks, as we were to find out, is quite another. Even on the lower slopes the jungle is dense, but higher up this is replaced by dense thickets of bamboo, through which, yard by weary back-breaking yard, we sometimes had to hack our way, making a trail sufficient for a mule carrying a wide load. To the north and south of this narrow valley, the mountains recede and give place to a wide valley, nowhere near as suitable for a road and rail block. With his acute eye for country, Wingate selected this narrow valley area as that in which he would block the road and railway. The hills, crowding in on the road and railway, offered lofty vantage points from which this vital line of communication could be dominated and also made it virtually impossible for any substantial amount of traffic to circumvent any road and rail block by going to one flank or the other. With Calvert and brigade headquarters went the 1st South Staffords and also the 3rd/6th Gurkha Rifles, one of whose columns was commanded by the diminutive but dynamic Freddie Shaw, whom we came greatly to admire, and 50 Column and 20 Column of the Lancashire Fusiliers, who were to act as flank guards and to "float" (that is, to act as a detached striking force), harrying any Japanese who attempted to approach or by-pass the block.

It took Calvert and his force six days to traverse the Gangaw Range and it was not until 16th March that they arrived at the site of the block (later to become known as "The White City" from the parachutes which festooned the trees) at the village of Henu, just north of Mawlu. Here the road and railway ran right along the edge of the hills skirting the east side of the valley - in fact at one point the road nudged into the lower part of the hills, and it had been identified from aerial photographs as forming an ideal spot for a road and rail block. A defensive position was laid out with its western flank following the road and rail for about 900 yards and extending eastwards about 300 or 400 yards to incorporate seven little hills which terminated abruptly along the southern flank of the perimeter, giving a view across low lying country to Mawlu, about a mile and a half further to the south. The South Staffords set about digging and wiring themselves in, and burrowing into the sides of the hills, a lengthy process which was protracted further because a supply drop of wire and tools which fell short had to be brought in.

The first enemy attack came on the night of the 17th March and was by two rifle companies led by Lt.Col Nagahashi, sent down from 18th Division. Most of them perished in the first few minutes of the attack and Nagahashi himself was mortally wounded. During the next three days there were further attacks from the enemy, not in great force, but sufficient to enable them to make a clearer appreciation of the strength of the defenders and when they realised that they had a really hard nut to crack, they withdrew for reinforcements.

In one of these actions, the brigadier personally initiated and led a bayonet charge to clear the enemy from the top of Pagoda Hill, at the south eastern corner of the block. With the Japs still holding the top of the Hill and the attack literally hanging in the balance, it was the brigadier's voice shouting "Come on now, one more effort, you've got them on the run!," which inspired the final desperate push putting the enemy to flight and, in the failing light, gave them possession of the hilltop.   The slopes were littered with the bodies of the foe, though fortunately our own dead were few but included one officer shot through the back of the head by a Japanese feigning to be dead.   During the ferocious hand to hand combat, Lieut. George Cairns of the South Staffords had his left arm hacked off by a Japanese officer. He shot the officer, picked up the Jap's sword with his remaining arm and laid about him at the enemy until he collapsed. For this gallant action he was awarded the Victoria Cross, the first of four to be earned by the Chindits during this campaign, but the last to be awarded because the original citation was lost in the air crash in which Wingate met his death.

WINGATE DIES IN AIR CRASH.

We had become quite used to visits from Wingate at Broadway. He came in his Mitchell bomber, wearing his old fashioned Wolseley sun helmet, crumpled bush jacket and trousers and dirty ammunition boots with a Lee Enfield rifle slung over his shoulder. We often wondered at his scruffy appearance, but it was quite obviously deliberately affected by him. He had only to say the word to be kitted out sprucely, as were most officers, let alone one of his senior rank. In many ways he was a character drawn straight out of the Old Testament, with his frequent quotations from that part of the Bible. He would have been well aware of the prophet Ezekiel, who at the beginning of his ministry, went to his fellow captives in Babylon and in silence "sat where they sat" for seven whole days to mark his total sympathy with them. I cannot help thinking that his appearance was part of a public relations exercise, aimed at the troops who almost revered him. He wanted them to be in no doubt that he, so to speak, "sat where they sat".

During the first World War, senior commanders often ran the War from gracious old French chateaux where they enjoyed an elegant lifestyle, remote from, although they controlled, the horror and carnage marked by the distant rumble of the guns and the constant flashes on the horizon. Not for Wingate this control from a distance. He wanted to be there where the action was and to be seen to be there - and I must admit that, no matter what his appearance, it gave us great comfort to see him there so frequently. From Broadway he visited the far flung columns by light plane, dispensing help, advice and encouragement. But this was so very soon and very tragically to end. On 24th March, he climbed into his Mitchell bomber at Broadway to return to base after one of his visits. He reached Imphal to confer with Air Marshal Baldwin, but taking off from there in bad weather he never reached home and a search discovered the burned out wreckage of his aircraft on a hillside in Assam, but there were no survivors. Lying some distance away, scorched and battered was his old Wolseley topi, which had been the object of so much silent ridicule, but which now identified him poignantly and far more effectively than any of the badly charred remains. When we heard the news, we found it difficult to believe that fate could have beén so cruel to deprive us of our leader less than three weeks into an operation which had enjoyed such great success. No matter who was appointed to succeed him, he could never be replaced and a sudden gloom descended upon us all.

For those of us who respected and admircd him as the great leader he undoubtedly was, and at the time were well nigh overwhelmed by the sense of loss, it is sad that so often when he is mentioned nowadays only some trivial or outlandish character-istic is associated with him. His true worth and qualities often seem to be submerged by this unfortunate patina. Mr. Winston Churchill, whose enjoyed not only unrivalled opportunities of meeting the greatest men of his era but also the sagacity to make a definitive judgment about them, spoke of Wingate in glowing terms:- "With him a bright flame was extinguished"...."Here was a man of genius, who might well have been also a man of destiny." Let his detractors remember these words and the source from whence they came.

Later we heard that Brigadier Joe Lentaigne of 111 Brigade had been appointed Force commander, but that meant little to us since we scarcely knew him. Though he would no doubt have been a very good choice for the command of the normal run of infantry divisions, he was not, from our standpoint, a good choice. He was not at all in tune with Wingate's ideas, he lacked his charisma and flair and, equally importantly his high ranking contacts (for which of course he couldn't be blamed) and also his "hands-on" control. In direct contrast to Wingate, he hardly ever visited his troops in the field, but was content to deal by remote control and he didn't have the weight required to stand up to General "Vinegar Joe" Stilwell, whose pathological hatred of all things British was legendary. As a consequence, in the closing stages of the campaign, the Chindits were remorselessly run into the ground, instead of being relieved.

With Lentaigne removed to higher things, the command of 111 Brigade surprisingly fell, not to one of the battalion commanders, but to the Brigade Major, Jack Masters, but without the rank of brigadier, which put him in an unusual and awkward position. I am open to correction on this, but I believe that Jumbo Morris, operating with Morrisforce on the Bhamo-Mytkyina road, took the rank but not the job. Jack Masters was later to become a world famous author with such books as - "The Road Past Mandalay"; "Bhowani Junction"; "Night Runners of Bengal"; "Bugles and a Tiger" and "The Deceivers" to mention but a few. He was the fifth generation of his family to have served in India and some of his earlier books, drawing upon this mightily impressive connection with the Raj, have an altogether extraordinary power to evoke the true atmosphere of India. He was a man of considerable intellect and the impression one gets from his later autobiographical books is that he reckoned himself destined to occupy the highest of ranks in the Army and, disillusioned not to have achieved this, he turned his back on England for the USA, eventually settling in New Mexico, where he died some years ago, sadly at an altogether too early age when he still had much to give to the world of letters.

Though those who knew him well spoke warmly of him, I did not find him a likeable person, when we later were transferred to his brigade, and that view seems to be shared by several of my old comrades. He seemed cool and distant, rather pompous and self opinionated - but maybe our joining his brigade so late in the campaign, making us in a sense "outsiders", had something to do with this.   For some, the heavy mantle of high rank and command rests easy on the shoulders and surely a supreme example of this must be General "Bill" Slim (later Field Marshal Viscount Slim), the commander of 14th Army, always regarded with affection by his men.   Perhaps Jack Masters found his particular mantle, assumed under most unusual and extremely testing circumstances, rather awkward and uncomfortable and this made him try too hard.   Perhaps he was just pre-occupied, and rightly so, with the immense problems which fell in upon him virtually without warning.

BATTLE AT BROADWAY.

On the evening of the 27th March, three days after Wingate's death, heavy firing broke out along the northern edge of our clearing, heralding the start of the enemy's ground attack. Our "D" company, commanded by Major Irwin Pickett was, so I believe, nominally fulfilling the role of "floater" company that night. In Chindit terminology a floater was a mobile striking force, able to attack any enemy which threatened or attacked the stronghold, the analogy being that of a hammer crushing a nut against the anvil of the stronghold. This concept was demonstrated very effectively by Calvert at The White City, where, leaving the road and rail block strongly held, he employed a separate force, comprised of two or more columns - eventually he had four battalions for this purpose - to harry the Japs in a wide area around the block, sometimes with the aid of fire from the 25 pounders located within the block and directed by radio by an artillery forward observation officer who accompanied the raiders.

In point of fact, however, "D" company was acting, on orders, more along the lines of a very large standing patrol, in position along the northern edge of the clearing, with 17 and 18 platoons to the west and company headquarters and 16 platoon to the east. With the benefit of hindsight, I find it difficult to understand how they came to be employed in this way and so close to our own perimeter. Warning of enemy approach could have been given much more effectively by a very small force, say a rifle section, who could have hit and run. If they were to be employed in a purely defensive role, they would have been more effective within our perimeter. If they were to act in a striking role, then I should have thought that they ought to have been well clear of our perimeter, so as not to be immediately embroiled in an attack on our position, but able to stand off and make their own decision as to when and where to hit the enemy, so as to achieve surprise and the maximum effect.

At 2240 hours a sentry of 18 platoon heard noises and opened fire. This drew a shower of grenades from the Japs, who had closed up undetected in strength. There followed a fierce battle which lasted for 40 minutes and with ammunition running low, and surrounded and greatly outnumbered by the enemy, the platoon was ordered to fall back on company HQ. In the confused melee which followed, the platoon commander, Jemadar Chandra Bahadur was killed with some stretcher bearers carrying one of their wounded comrades. Finding their way back to company HQ blocked by the enemy, the remainder of the platoon took cover in the thickets and awaited an opportunity to return to the stronghold. The enemy attack then flowed on and engulfed company HQ and 16 platoon. Time and again they charged, but were beaten back.

Sadly Irwin Pickett was mortally wounded by an enemy grenade which exploded in his lap. Subedar Indra Bahadur took charge and, as ammunition ran low, in a splendid demonstration of resolution and courage, he had all the spare hand grenades collected and passed to him and as each enemy attack came in, he personally threw each of the grenades so that none was wasted, but each was used to maximum effect in inflicting casualties on the enemy, who greatly outnumbered them. In the pitch black darkness of the night, ferocious hand to hand encounters took place, with kukhris, bayonets, rifle butts and boots being employed in desperation until our men managed to break contact and vanish into the jungle, to regroup and make their way back to the stronghold as best they could.

The attack against "D" company then eased off and in the silence that followed, we heard what appeared to be a working party returning from the airstrip, though well appreciating that no working party could possibly be abroad in those circumstances. On the front held by "B" company, a salient of jungle, about 20 yards wide, projected out westwards into the clearing just north of the airstrip. The "working party" marched up to the northern face of this salient to crisp commands in English - "Left, right, left right.....Halt!....Right turn!"...Then screaming in unison "Charge!".. and our password, which was "Mandalay", they came at us.

I am puzzled as to what they expected to achieve by this hollow subterfuge, because, having learnt our lessons in the Arakan, strict fire discipline was observed and our formal welcome, rowdy and rumbustious, was reserved until they hit our wire. Though they took heavy casualties, a couple of the more enterprising of them actually got through our wire and were killed a couple of yards inside it, one of them by a grenade truckled along the ground which had exploded under his chin. It hadn't blown his head off, but had splayed out his bottom jaw and the bottom part of his face, giving him a bizarre frog-like appearance. Implacable and ruthless enemy he might have been, but he was also a very brave man and he and many of his comrades had to be awarded full marks for sheer guts and determination. They were travelling very light and, looking inside their haversacks, we found that the only rations they carried were a sock full of rice and a handful of raw brown sugar wrapped in a piece of brown paper.

At first light, as the survivors of "D" company tried to make their way back with their wounded, they came under enemy fire and Major R.E.G. ("Reggie") Twelvetrees took out a platoon of "A" company and brought them back, together with Irwin's body. After the manner of our riflemen, he had had the top of his head shaven, except for a very small area right at the crown of the head, where the hair had been allowed to grow in a long tuft. Our men believed that when they died in battle, this tuft enabled the gods to snatch their soul up into heaven. We had often "ribbed" Irwin about this, and as I saw the top of his head, above the blanket which covered his lifeless form, I felt sorry if we had ever embarrassed him about this, but silently offered up a little prayer that God might in fact have snatched his soul up into heaven. In a simple little ceremony, we buried him just outside the south eastern corner of the perimeter.

Later that morning Reggie took out another fighting patrol from his company. They closed undetected upon 35 Japs and went in with kukhri and bayonet, killing 16 Japs for the loss of 2 of our men killed and 7 wounded. Our own losses for this first brush with the enemy at Broadway were 50 killed and wounded of which about three quarters had been wounded. Andy Rebori and his light plane pilots had been our unwilling guests at this fireworks show. Some of them had not thought it necessary to dig slit trenches, no doubt preferring the comfort of their jungle hammocks to the slog of wielding pick and shovel, but oddly enough, they seemed to have had a change of mind! Indeed had anyone been engaged on a time and motion study on the important subject of digging slit trenches, they would have had an opportunity of collecting some useful data.

Coming under Jap machine-gun fire for the first time would have spurred them to additional effort. I had found it puzzling. Splinters were punched out of the trees just above your head as the bullets struck home, but what was unsettling was that it sounded as if the machine-gun itself was being fired at you point-blank from that very spot. In those far off days, scientific knowledge now regarded as commonplace was not enjoyed by most of us, and it was not until years later that I was able to work out that the bullets must have been travelling at a speed in excess of the speed of sound and that we were hearing a super sonic boom as each passed overhead. The Jap bullet was of smaller calibre and higher velocity than our own, but if it hit anything solid, like bone, it tended to turn turtle and inflict a larger wound.

During a break in the fighting, our light plane pilots, taking the view that Broadway was no longer tenable as a light plane base, took off in some of the planes which had not been damaged and left us for Aberdeen. Later our own two attached RAF officers were to find that they could make at least two of the remaining planes airworthy and were able to use them extensively. At first we thought it surprising that the Japs had not done a more effective job of destroying the planes, but it could well be that they were so confident of evicting us that they wanted to preserve them for use by their own pilots. A similar concept was applied in regard to equipment in areas overrun on the other fronts - do not destroy needlessly, preserve for possible use.

For the next few days, enemy attacks continued, mostly at night and I remember one night in particular. There was an electrical storm of an intensity I don't think I've ever experienced before or since. There was continuous incessant thunder and lightning, with the rain bucketing down almost as if you were under a waterfall and a near hurricane force wind, which brought great branches crashing down upon us from the canopy high above our heads. As if this were not enough, the Japs attacked under cover of a massive mortar bombardment, our own mortars were firing, showers of grenades were being exchanged accompanied by intense rifle and machine-gun fire and screams and shouts from both sides . It seemed as if the Almighty and his creatures were all engaged in a desperate contest to see who could make the most noise and cause the greatest mayhem.

I decided to go and see how my own lads were getting on and was crawling on my hands and knees along a shallow and narrow communications trench and putting my head up from time to time to look around, because it seemed to me that the Japs were likely to get through the wire and come flooding over us at any moment. In all the noise and tumult it was quite impossible to hear a mortar bomb falling (as we usually managed to do). As I stopped and raised my head to look over the top, two mortar bombs landed absolutely simultaneously and within three feet of me, on either side of the trench. I felt a crashing, stunning blow across the top and back of my head, as if some giant hand had taken a mighty swipe at me, which knocked me violently face down in the mud at the bottom of the trench. A split second later and the whole of my head would have been right in line with the explosions, and I just don't see how I could have survived. I found myself vomiting and retching uncontrollably and, though I struggled as hard as I could to get control of myself, many minutes passed before I managed to do so. I suppose I must have been suffering from a combination of concussion and shell-shock, but I was in good physical condition and very resilient psychologically and, in the relief of still being alive, was soon able to shake off the after effects of my experience, though it has left my hearing impaired.

Despite the ferocity of their attacks, the enemy never again managed to penetrate our defences. With them they had brought a large number of coolies to remove the dead, regarding this as ritually important. One of these coolies managed to escape and take refuge inside the perimeter, two days after the attack began. He proved to be a Captain Chai Shuh-Ming, of the Chinese military intelligence service, who had been captured some time before, but being able to speak Burmese had passed himself off as a coolie. He told us that our attackers were a weak battalion of the 146th Regiment of the 56th Division commanded by Major Wakayuma, that in their attack on us they had already lost 100 men, including the battalion's second in command. Before we finally parted company with them, that casualty list was to grow.

Our fighting patrols combing the jungle, came under fire from Jap snipers in the tree tops and Jemadar Yem Bahadur Sahi and his men proved expert in spotting and dealing with them. Lt. Col.

Walter Scott D.S.O., M.C., who had greatly distinguished himself in Operation Longcloth, was operating with his two columns of the 1st Bn. The King's Regiment - Column 81 under his command and Column 82 commanded by Major Gaitley, outside our perimeter to offer us such help as they could.   On 30th March, Col. Rome, in command at Broadway, called for help, but our radios, designed mainly to communicate direct with Base, were not always reliable in lateral contact with another column and the message was picked up only by Gaitley. He had just had a heavy battle with a Jap company and was able to send only a strong fighting patrol under command of Captain Coultart. They attacked from the west towards our perimeter but were badly cut up and Coultart, a good and brave officer, was killed. The survivors of the patrol, shaken and rattled, joined us inside the wire.

On 31st March we were lucky enough to obtain air support and as our fighter bombers circled immediately overhead in their "cab rank", we spoke with them over our radio and indicated the enemy position by a coloured smoke bomb from one of our 3" mortars.   One after another they swept in and dropped their bombs with a highly satisfying crump, and we felt the ground heave below us from the massive explosions nearby. Clambering out of our trenches, we made our way through the wire and advanced in open order, through the clouds of dust and smoke raised by the bombing, expecting any moment to come under fire from the enemy - but at the approach of the bombers they had fled, leaving their positions deserted. In front of one of their weapon pits I saw something which filled me with rage and despair. The bodies of seven of our men had been stacked in a pile about two or three feet high, all aligned in the same direction as if they were nothing more than a pile of logs and it was obvious that they had been taken prisoner and then butchered mercilessly. A rifle section had been posted in a bunker, just outside the south western corner of our perimeter, as a guard on the light plane bays. At the start of the enemy attack they had sent back a runner to say that they were under attack and running short of ammunition, but would hold on as long as they could. These were the bodies of the brave men from that rifle section, and it was just another instance of the barbarity of the Japs.

Thereafter on patrol around the northern edge of the jungle, we came from time to time on the headless body of one of our men, bloated and infested with flies, and a few feet away a blackened head also in an advanced stage of putrefaction - obviously luckless men of "D" company who had been captured and beheaded to afford a Japanese officer some sword practice on a living target. Such were just some of our experiences of the vaunted Japanese concept of "Bushido", and thousands of similar or much worse experiences could be related by anyone who had anything to do with the Japanese during the war. It is not at all surprising that so many of our men who fought against the Japanese are of the view that whatever came to the Japanese later by way of horror and retribution, no-one deserved it or earned it more than they.

There followed a period when we were no longer molested by the enemy - they had obviously found us too tough a nut to crack by the application of forces readily available and, with so much else to cope with, could not afford to employ the special effort which would be needed to dislodge us. We therefore continued with the task originally allotted to us, running the stronghold and extensively patrolling the country round about us. By now the Chindits had really made their presence felt and in his book, Louis Allen says that a special army group, 33 Army Group comprising 18, 53 and 56 Divisions and 24 Independent Mixed Brigade, with its headquarters at Maymyo had been specially formed to deal with the menace posed by the Chindits and Stilwell's forces. So much for Mutaguchi's initial - "they're only a mouse in a bag!" - reaction.

During this "quiet" period our two attached RAF officers experienced a new lease of life. Casting aside for a time the bonds of earth, they were often aloft in two of the light planes which were now in service once again solely as a result of their considerable mechanical skill in using replacement parts obtained from some of the other planes. They ranged far and wide on patrol and also indulged themselves in aerobatic displays.

One day I found myself involved in an aerial foray, which perhaps fortunately did not achieve its full purpose. The brigade major came to see me and suggested that we should both use the light planes to go on a bombing mission!. The plan though at first sight somewhat implausible was quite simple and straight forward. We would stuff the front of our shirts with grenades, sally aloft, locate the enemy and then just drop the hand grenades on top of them. I must confess to having some misgivings about the plan, but the brigade major was a man of immense charm to say nothing of great seniority both in rank and service - so what could I do but bury any niggling doubts!. Our RAF comrades entered into the spirit of the operation, or should I say escapade, and soon we were aloft in two separate light aircraft flying side by side, our weighty load of grenades making us look vaguely like a couple of heavily pregnant women, though a stray bullet hitting them could have blown us to kingdom come.

Below us in the long soft shadows cast by the light of the rising sun, the countryside was ineffably beautiful as we headed in a generally westerly direction. The steep sided hills of the Gangaw Range, densely covered in verdant jungle, climbed up towards us and marched away in serried ranks into the bluey greys of the distance whilst the morning mists still swirled in the valleys. Before long we were to traverse the Range on foot and those hills and valleys would impose back breaking hours and days of toil and strain, but for the moment I was entranced by the overwhelming joyous wonder of it all. There can be few places on earth more beautiful than Burma, but generally we were at the disadvantage of viewing it under adverse conditions. We were flying well to the north of the White City and, in my view mercifully, did not locate any enemy patrols. Almost as bad, we located a British column which I think had probably come out from Aberdeen. As they waved their hats and arms at us in token of glad recognition, our pilots responded with a series of aerobatics which I suppose was the RAF equivalent of a feu de joie. As I gazed over the pilot's shoulder in mesmerized disbelief I found myself hurtling vertically downwards and pulling out of the dive at the very last moment as it appeared to me that we were almost certain to crash. The roar of the engine prevented us from hearing what our friends and comrades on the ground were saying as they scattered hither and thither in alarm, but my military training enabled me to hazard what was probably an accurate guess!. We soared upwards to loop the loop, put in a couple of victory rolls and then swept low a few times over our admiring friends on the ground before heading for home.

It had all been too much for me and I felt very ill. The brigade major, made of sterner stuff, grinned hugely across the intervening airspace and waved at us. Averting my face I waved back in what I hoped might be regarded as a nonchalant manner before being sick in as genteel a fashion as I could contrive. Back at base I tottered feebly out of the plane, the unexpended portion of the day's grenade ration clunking hollowly around my empty midriff. Though outwardly sympathetic, I could sense that the pilot was not very pleased and the upshot of the matter was that I was not allowed, either literally or figuratively to darken the door of his aircraft ever again.

WHITE CITY - SUCCESS SURRENDERED

White City had been turned into a virtually impregnable fortress. Calvert kept all at work on the defences which became a maze of slit trenches and bunkers dug and burrowed into the hill sides and roofed in with heavy timbers which rendered them proof against anything but a direct hit from a heavy artillery shell. Lt. Col Richards the C.O. of the South Staffs had been killed in the early stages of establishing the block and I was greatly saddened to learn of his death. He was a small dapper man of great personal charm, not a bit like the blood and thunder image of a Chindit leader, but he was mortally wounded whilst personally leading a counter attack against the Japs with great gallantry. His place was taken by his second in command, Ron Degg, a tough former coal miner, who had risen from the ranks and commanded the battalion with great distinction. Calvert already had three battalions with him at the White City, and Lentaigne sent him three more by way of reinforcements - two Nigerians, the 7th and 12th and also the 45th Reconnaissance Regiment. Later the 6th Battalion of the Nigerian Regiment was also sent to him so that he had the equivalent of two brigades under command. The Nigerians, who, as previously related, had blotted their copy book by running into an ambush, soon redeemed their reputation and Calvert thought highly of them. Three battalions were used to man the block and the others were used as a mobile force of marauders.

By 27th March a team of USAAF engineers had arrived by glider, with equipment to construct an airstrip on the far side of the railway and about 400 yards from the block for the use of

Dakotas, to supplement the light plane strip on the near side of the railway. They then flew in four 25 pounder field guns, six 40mm Bofors anti aircraft guns and four 2 pounder anti tank guns and installed them in the block. From then on it was possible to supply the block by Dakota instead of by airdrop. The defences were strengthened and minefields laid in front of the wire. The Japs routinely shelled and mortared the block by night and sent in air raids by day, but the Bofors teams did splendid work, on one occasion shooting down five aircraft, all verified, during a single raid. One of the enemy mortars fired a huge bomb, 150mm in diameter, 5 feet long and weighing 200lbs which exploded with an horrendous noise, which could be heard quite clearly by Fergusson at Aberdeen, 25 miles away. Fortunately it was not very lethal.

When General-Kawabe realised the weight and thrust of the Chindit offensive he was greatly alarmed. Things were not going well with Mutaguchi's attack on Imphal, where 100,000 of his best troops were locked in battle, and within a few days, the tide of conflict would flow in favour of the defenders. The official British records put the turning point at 15th April. The troops available to him to meet this new threat were not of the same calibre, nor were his generals. The elite 18th Division - "The Chrysanthemums" - were committed in combat with Stilwell and, though well under strength, greatly resented taking reinforcements from inferior units. Kawabe brought up the 24th Independent Brigade commanded by Colonel Hyashi and made its strength up to eight battalions (known as "Take Force") as opposed to Calvert's seven, and they dug themselves in around Mawlu and set about softening up the block.

With his force outside the block, Calvert ranged far and wide. Patrols were sent out to intercept any mule trains which tried to circumvent the block by using the trails in the hills, convoys on the road south of the block were ambushed and Capt. Nicholls, from his lookout on the top of O.P.Hill, brought the fire of his 25 pounders to bear on suitable targets. Air strikes were directed on to enemy positions. They were subjected to 500 lb bombs, cannon fire from the Mustangs, shells from the 75mm guns carried by the bombers and occasionally the thunderclaps of parachute bombs, which burst overhead, projecting a death dealing cloud of shrapnel over a wide area. A patrol found a despairing letter from a Jap officer saying that flesh and blood could not stand up to these air attacks and that, unless something could be done about them, the whole operation was doomed. Frequent ground attacks were made on enemy positions, but these were greatly hampered by the profusion of tenacious lantana scrub which thickly covered hundreds of acres of the ground.

Night after night, from the 6th April, the enemy tried to force their way into the block, attempting to cut the wire with Bangalore torpedoes (long pipes filled with explosives) or to climb over the wire and swamp the mines by sheer weight of numbers. The sixteen 3" mortars were all trained on to the perimeter, these and every other available weapon were brought to bear on the attackers and even the Bofors depressed their barrels and fired pointblank. After a pause, the attack would be repeated again in exactly the same spot in a senseless, totally unimaginative way. The only result was to add further corpses to the hundreds hanging in the wire or lying in the minefields. They lay there bloated, rotting and stinking, covered with clouds of gorged flies and quite inaccessible for burial. Attempts to cremate them with flamethrowers only substituted one revolting stench and sight for another. The light plane pilots said that they used to navigate by smell. On their arrival, one of the Nigerian battalions relieved the 3rd/6th Gurkhas in the block, releasing them for Calvert's force. On their first night they were horror stricken, but soon settled in and became a formidable part of the defence force.

Surprisingly, Hyashi never tried to hem in the block, or to deny it its air supplies by use of his own anti-aircraft guns, but pressed home his senseless attacks night after night without success. On

17th April he made one last desperate throw, this time by day instead of by night, under cover of an intense artillery bombardment. Suicide groups with Bangalore torpedoes made a wide breach in the wire and the Japanese swarmed up O.P. Hill, where the gunner's observation post was sited. The platoon of the South Staffs defending the hill hung on with grim determination and with only sixteen out of its forty men still standing. This gave the Nigerians a chance to put in a counter attack. In savage and confused hand to hand combat, the intruders were eliminated one by one and the last of the Japs was killed by a Nigerian wielding a heavy box of hand grenades by its rope handle. Hyashi, ·leading the assault, was killed on the horse he had ceremoniously mounted for the occasion, as in the true bushido spirit, he deliberately elected to mark his failures by dying with his men.

General Takeda then took over command of the survivors of Take Force and wisely decided to defer any further attacks on the block until the whole of his 53rd Division were assembled and ready. Indeed, subdued if not downright cowed by what had happened, Take Force made no move at all against the block between the 18th April and 11th May. By that time, it was too late, since much against Calvert's wishes, the block had on Lentaigne's orders been evacuated and replaced by another block to the North near Hopin, to be known as "Blackpool". The evacuation was a thoroughly impudent affair, staged at very considerable risk for public relations purposes.

On the night of the 9th May, with the Japanese only two miles away, a total of forty Dakotas loaded with supplies landed on the strip and three of them were redirected to Broadway to assist in the flyout there. The rest were loaded up with the sick and wounded, all the guns and stores and the sick and surplus mules, who seemed to sense what was afoot since they lost all their inhibitions about boarding transport and jostled with each other and their drivers to board the planes. Although a battalion were shooting up the Japs around Mawlu, to distract them, it just did not seem possible that they would allow this intense air activity to take place without interference and those on the airstrip spent two nerve wracking hours expecting any moment to come under intense artillery fire.   After all, the enemy guns had already carefully registered on the block and airstrip and the Jap gunners could easily have laid their guns and opened fire.   But no intervention came and Chindits left, cock-a-hoop that they had pulled off this blatantly cheeky operation without loss or even challenge.

FROM BROADWAY TO BLACKPOOL.

Early in May, Noel George fell ill and had to be evacuated and only much later did we learn with sadness that he had contracted poliomyelitis. To replace him, Alec Harper who had been with Morrisforce was flown in by light plane on 8th May. He was a cavalryman from the famous Indian regiment, The Deccan Horse, who had volunteered for service with Special Force to see some action, but had never served with Gurkhas, apart from his brief spell with the 4th/9th Gurkhas in Morrisforce. We therefore felt a little apprehensive as to how he would fit in, coming from a background so very different from our own, but we need not have worried. He soon exerted his influence and proved to be well versed in infantry tactics and jungle warfare and someone who led us incisively and with great skill and determination. We were very fortunate indeed to have him.

It was decided that Broadway had fulfilled its purpose and should be abandoned. All surplus stores and equipment were back loaded to Assam by Dakota flights which came in for that purpose and we put ourselves on the required operational basis to enable us to function as two separate columns - numbered 57 and 93, one commanded by Alec Harper and the other by Reggie Twelvetrees. All British and Gurkha officers were issued with the American M30 carbine, a great improvement on the old .303 Lee Enfield rifle which some of us had toted around. It was short and much lighter than our rifles, its magazine held 15 rounds and it was semi-automatic. Although the cartridge was much smaller and the bullet lighter and it was therefore not as good as our rifles for long range work, it could be, with its semi-automatic action, very deadly for close quarter action - and many of the engagements in the jungle fell into that category. One day, later on, our Burma Rifles officer, Bill Hardless bumped straight into a party of three Japs and before they could sort themselves out, he despatched all three of them with his carbine. I traded my .38 Smith & Wesson revolver for one of the light plane pilot's .45 Remington automatic pistol - it took Tommy gun ammunition of which we had a good stock and I reasoned that this hard hitting weapon would be far more likely to stop a charging Jap in his tracks than my regulation .38 S & W, though the automatic was far more likely to jam than the revolver. I don't suppose I'm likely to be court martialled after all this time!

Even a revolver is not entirely fail safe. Norman Durant, of the South Staffs, taking part in the attack on Pagoda Hill at White City, raced up the hillside but as he rounded the corner of a building ran slap into a party of Japs with rifles and fixed bayonets charging down hill towards him - the leading two were just twenty yards away and looking distinctly unfriendly. His platoon sergeant, carrying a Sten gun and followed by a couple of his men, were still 30 yards behind and around the corner out of sight. He levelled his revolver at them and pressed the trigger - but nothing happened (it later transpired that the hammer had worked loose). In his other hand he had a grenade, so he pulled out the pin and lobbed the grenade behind the Japs, did a terrific swerve to the left and took a flying leap over the hillside and, as he did so, felt a violent blow on his knee and knew he'd been hit. By this time, his men had rounded the corner, killed the two leading Japs and taken on the others, who were disorientated by the grenade.

We each stocked up with five days supply of the infamous "K" ration, three cartons for each day, marked "Breakfast", "Dinner" and "Supper". Breakfast comprised instant coffee, powdered milk, a tin of cheese with small flecks of ham, biscuits, sugar and a date bar. Dinner was tinned spam, lemonade powder, biscuits, chocolate and a fruit bar.   Supper was similar but with soup powder instead of lemonade. Each packet also contained four cigarettes. To save space, we opened the cartons, discarded them and stowed all the other items in our packs. On the march, "brewing up" normally had to be done before first light and after dark, so that the smoke did not give away our position, and our orderlies made individual fires with a few twigs, combining the biscuits, soup and spam etc. to make a sort of hash, which though not exactly cordon bleu, went down fairly well after a strenuous day on the trail. Those of us who baulked at the monotony of the menu, and most of us did from time to time, had to force ourselves to eat just to keep the essential energy quotient going in. There were to be times when we starved for days on end and then longed for our hated rations again. We had to subsist on these rations for months on end, but they were really formulated to be used as an emergency ration only and for only about ten days at a time, and no doubt this was one of the main contributory factors to increasing ill health amongst us as the campaign dragged on. Sometimes a supply drop would contain fresh bread, butter and jam, but this would be devoured voraciously in one meal.

In the early morning of 13th May we headed for the Railway Valley and said goodbye to Broadway for the last time, leaving it via a gap in the wire in the south eastern corner of the perimeter, quite close to Irwin Pickett's grave and so moved straight into the jungle instead of into the clearing. As we did so, we traversed a shallow dry nullah bed and just to the left of the line of march, I saw a wonderful sight which has remained, etched in my memory. In a small patch of the nullah bed, not much more than a yard square, were packed a great mass of butterflies of the most beautiful hues - there seemed to be hundreds of them. I spotted them as we entered the nullah and swivelled my head to keep them in my gaze as we marched the dozen paces or so across the width of the nullah - and then they were gone leaving just a lustrous memory to carry with me through the years. I had not the slightest idea of what made them settle there in such profusion, and, of course, march discipline precluded any investigation.

Following the narrow trail in an immensely long, snaking single file, we soon forded the Kaukkwe Chaung and headed for the Gangaw Range, each carrying a load of about sixty pounds including our rations, equipment, weapons , spare ammunition and about six grenades. Setting off in the cool of the morning, the load, though heavy, seemed tolerable but as the heat and humidity increased and the straps of your pack and equipment cut into your shoulders, you began to look forward more and more to the ten or five minute break at the end of each hour's marching. You tended to lean forward into the weight of your pack and to develop what was known as "the Chindit stoop".

With all its men and animals, a double column battalion could extend for over a mile down the jungle track and there was a special bivouac drill to get everyone into harbour for the night. The head of the column would go off the track and, taking a course at right angles to the track, proceed straight into the jungle for about four hundred yards and select say a suitably imposing tree or a small valley as H.Q. As the first rifle company came in, it would be sent out on a bearing of zero degrees and would follow that bearing for a couple of hundred yards or more, depending on the density of the jungle or any special physical features on the ground and would treat that point as the centre of the front of his company position. A screen of sentries would then be sent forward about another hundred yards into the jungle and, behind this screen the company commander would lay out his company's position for the night, probably having two of his platoons forward and one in reserve and would feel out to his right and left flanks to link up with the companies coming in there.

As the second company came in it would be sent out on a bearing of 120 degrees and the third on a bearing of 240 degrees, each then following the same drill as the first company and the fourth would probably be held in reserve around battalion H.Q., having dropped off a standing patrol near the point where the columns had left the main track. The "thin red line" was quite definitely out. Every company's position would be laid out in depth, in a series of individual weapon pits, dug as well as time permitted and sited so that each could give covering fire to the others. An enemy attack coming through the perimeter would therefore encounter an integrated defensive position,hundreds of yards in depth, comprised of numerous individual strongpoints.

Meanwhile, at battalion H.Q., an aerial would be thrown up into the tree and radio contact established with base. The "chore horse", a small petrol driven battery charger, would be started to keep the batteries topped up and incoming and outgoing messages would have to be deciphered or enciphered. One of the most familiar sounds around H.Q. was that of the chore horse and the morse key. If a supply drop were required, the date time and place had to be determined and passed to base, together with the requisition for the stores needed, but individual items did not need to be spelled out, since we had a coded inventory to simplify the process. Each day two separate rendezvous had to be determined and promulgated - the near rendezvous where we would be at the end of the day and the distant rendezvous, where we expected to be say in three or four days time. We were under constant threat of ambush or of having to meet the enemy in a hard fought action, in which some of our men might be scattered and not be able to regroup immediately and it was therefore essential for everyone to know how they could link up with the main body again.

The unsung - and unsinging - heroes of the campaign were undoubtedly our mules. Unsinging, because they had been de-voiced, their vocal chords had been severed to prevent them from braying and giving away our presence, thus, no doubt, depriving them of one of their main pleasures in life. On hardly any hard feed at all and just what they could forage from the jungle, they kept on and on, valiant and stout hearted to the end. Occasionally you would see them in "light hearted" mood, cantering away, bucking as they went, scattering their loads in all directions and dragging their cursing muleteers around on the end of their bridles as if they were of no weight at all.

As we left Broadway, we were joined by quite a remarkable young Irishman named Bill Smyly. He was a veteran of Operation Longcloth, when he had been Animal Transport Officer with Bernard Fergusson's column. Not content with that very rough and tough experience, he had managed to join Fergusson's brigade in the present operation, but when they came to Broadway to be flown out, still not satisfied, and hearing that we were going to be engaged in some fighting, he obtained Fergusson's permission to join our battalion as we marched off to the Railway Valley. In effect, he was trying to fit three separate campaigns into two years - an enthusiasm which few of us shared! He loved his mules and despite spending all his working hours with our recalcitrant friends, he was always cheerful and composed. He was, I think, by far the youngest of us and if not still in his teens, had only just left them. Though animal management was his strong point, spelling was not, but suspect spelling must not be allowed to overshadow the sagacity of something which, according to Fergusson, he wrote on the subject of crossing rivers with mules. "With regard to river-crossing," wrote Bill, "there are three tipes of mules. The first tipe will go quitely, if they have good mulatiers. The second tipe have to be ceduced. For the third tipe, there is nothing for it but WRAPE!"

We struggled slowly on, up the slopes of the Gangaw Range, often in the pelting rain and along a track which soon deteriorated into a sea of mud churned up by the mules and men ahead of us. Sometimes we had to leave the track and hack our way laborious-ly through dense thickets of bamboo and other profuse undergrowth, chopping with dahs and kukhris a path wide enough to permit the passage of a mule with panniers or other loads across its back. Sometimes the path climbed steeply up or down, where the mules, blowing hard, struggled to get a footing in the slippery mud, the steam rising in clouds from their heaving, sweating flanks from their exertions under their heavy loads, their sweating muleteers hauling on their heads and beating the hindquarters of the animal ahead of them, to get them to move. With the straps of our packs and equipment cutting into our shoulders and our backs almost breaking under our loads, we fared no better than our animals as we struggled to keep our balance in the slippery, cloying mud which denied a secure purchase to our leading foot and yet refused to let go of our rear foot, as we sought to free it and place it in front of the other. The sweat trickled down our faces and backs and dropped steadily from the tip of our noses as, panting with exertion we grabbed with one hand or the other at any convenient branch or bush to steady ourselves. Occasionally you would miss your footing, or slip in the mud and end up on your hands and knees, under your sixty pounds load, and then have to drag yourself painfully to your feet once again and carry on once more.

At the end of such a day, to reach the night bivouac and to lay down your pack and equipment for the last time for the day, was like reaching the portals of heaven itself. But it was not just a case of lying down and putting your feet up. There was always so much to do before you could at last relax. Behind your back though, you could hear your Gurkha officer "organising" your orderly to lay out your gear and your "bed" space (maybe it would be little more than a bundle of bamboo shoots under your groundsheet to make the ground not quite so hard) and also getting your evening meal in train, glancing the meanwhile out of the corner of his eye to satisfy himself that you were alright and generally acting like an old hen, protecting you, his solitary chick.

The Gurkha officers were an exceptional breed of men, the very salt of the earth, they held the Viceroy's commission and were therefore sometimes referred to as "V.C.Os" (you of course held the King's commission). They had worked their way up through the ranks and held their present rank not just by virtue of long service, but as a result of outstanding ability. In a rifle company, each of the three platoons was commanded by a "jemedar" and above them in the command structure was the company "subedar" and there were also two British officers, the company commander with the rank of major and the company officer, usually a lieutenant. Headquarters Company with its support groups - mortar platoon, machine-gun platoon, signal platoon and animal transport - was organised similarly.

Then, in battalion H.Q., there was the jemedar adjutant, who assisted the adjutant, and also the subedar major, the most senior Gurkha officer in the battalion. The "S.M.", as we called him, was one of the most, if not the most important man in the battalion; he was a confidant of the colonel and a diplomat to his finger tips and nearly always he and the colonel had grown up together in the battalion and knew it and its men inside out. They were on such good terms with each other that, without in any way ceding proper respect and discipline, they could each speak his mind to the other, knowing that any confidences would not be betrayed. In this way any matters of concern could be properly aired and dealt with before causing any real problem. The S.M. and his fellow Gurkha officers thus formed an essential link between the British officers and the whole of the rest of the battalion. The Gurkhas were very "choosey" and perceptive about their British officers and demanded high standards of them and,if they were not entirely satisfied, the word edged its way up the chain of command, if in fact the deficiency had not already been perceived by the senior British officers, - and there were always postings of one sort or another which had to be filled by some British officer or the other!

If you passed their test, you found yourself almost embarrassingly elevated into a position almost akin to that of a demi-god, surrounded by wealth of loyalty, support and simple affection which you knew you did not really merit. They were fiercely protective of you, and if in a rare exchange of confidences, one of your men told you he would lay down his life for you - and that has happened to me - you knew that he was not shooting a line but just making a plain and greatly humbling statement of fact. The effect on you was the reverse to what might have been expected - it didn't make you big headed, but resolute that, come hell or high water, you would not let such men down or prove unworthy of such trust. All the men had very similar names. Their second name was nearly always "Bahadur" (brave) or sometimes "Singh" (lion) and nobody lived up to those names more than they. They had a third name, their tribal name such as "Chhettri" or "Thapa" or "Gurung", which wasn't used so frequently. If you called "Kim Bahadur" or "Kesh Bahadur" or "Gupta Bahadur" for example, you might have three or four men responding, if it wasn't absolutely clear who was meant. The men therefore used to hail each other by using the last two ciphers in their regimental number, e.g."pacchis" (25), "das" (10)and so on - my former orderly Gupta Bahadur was "panch" (05) and later was to win the Military Medal for outstanding bravery in the attack on Point 2171, where Jimmy Blaker was to win his Victoria Cross.

On the fourth day of our march we came to the village of Lamai, set on a spur high up in the Gangaw Range, hemmed in by the mountains to the north and west but not far from the western flank of the Range. Here we stayed for 24 hours waiting for the supply drop we'd arranged and learned from the brigadier that we were to be transferred to 111 Brigade at the new road and rail block, codenamed "Blackpool", near Namkwin railway station. Taking a supply drop in the hills was always an uncertain exercise at this time of the year, when low lying cloud could obscure the dropping zone and put the low flying aircraft at risk of crashing into the hillside. On a number of occasions,in difficult weather conditions, we would "talk" the pilot down on our radio, only to hear him say that he dare not come down any lower and since he still could not see us, he would just have to return to base, without making the drop. We were then left without rations, supplies and ammunition to fend for ourselves as best we could. On this day however the weather was good and hearing the drone of the aircraft, we fired a Verey light and the plane made a straight run over the top of us and a great cascade of parachutes came tumbling out and then floating down gracefully towards us, to be collected and checked at top speed and the contents distributed. Not all the parachutes landed on the dropping zone. Some had to be collected from the trees, where this was possible, and we kept a special lookout for the red parachute, which brought down the mail. The parachutes themselves were greatly prized by the villagers for the large quantity of material which they contained and, where possible, were passed on to them.

From Lamai the track descended steeply down the top of the spur, in a generally westerly direction, to Loilaw and then hugged the foothills on the western flank of the Gangaw Range, going south west to Hkinlap.   After two days we were there and contemplating, from the fringes of the jungle, the last short stage of the journey to the block at Blackpool, just four miles away due west across the open paddy fields of the Railway Valley. It was obvious that this could be a particularly hazardous part of the journey, when we would be right out in the open, vulnerable to an enemy attack from the south up the valley, where the enemy could now move quite freely no longer impeded by the block at White City, or down the valley from the north, where there never had been any block. The nascent block at Blackpool was having its own problems, as we were shortly to discover. Just across the valley we could see the shadowy outline of the eastern foothills of the Bumrawng Bum (the Bumrawng massif), where Blackpool had been tenuously established.

Calvert had assured Alec that - "In the daylight the valley is ours. You can go where you like." So, taking a very careful look, we formed up, abandoning the long winding snake formation we'd followed so long, and launched ourselves from the jungle, in close column of companies in extended order. Along our front flowed the Namyin Chaung which, gathering all the streams and rivers from the great watersheds of both the western flanks of the Gangaw range and the eastern flanks of the Bumrawng Bum, flowed northwards to the Mogaung River. We had no difficulty in making the crossing, but within a matter of hours the rains were to set in and the Namyin was to become an impassable, violent, raging torrent, flooding over its banks to the width of a mile and isolating 77 Brigade from any defensive action in support of Blackpool. The grand strategy, if it can be so called, was also to be frustrated, as much by the forces of nature as by those of the enemy.

BLACKPOOL ESTABLISHED BUT EMBATTLED.

Calvert and his stout-hearted band of men, sadly depleted in numbers by battle casualties from the almost incessant fighting under his inspiring leadership and also, increasingly by illness, had been required by Stilwell to make one last effort to assist him in taking Mogaung from the Japs. He had protested about this and continued to protest vigorously about the scandalous abandonment of White City, established and maintained so effectively by his men at such a great cost in blood and materials. In his excellent and comprehensive book on the çampaign called "The Chindit War", Brigadier Shelford Bidwell says that Calvert's protests were made so publicly that Lentaigne, overcoming his dislike for personal confrontation, called him to a conference at Broadway on 8th May and there patiently reasoned with him and explained that they were under Stilwell's command and had to obey his orders and added that if Calvert still felt that he could not comply, then he would have to be relieved of command of his brigade. Calvert saw sense - many years later he was to admit that he "had been getting too big for his boots" - and Lentaigne was spared the anguish of having to dismiss his bravest and most able brigadier. It seems to me however, that as the plans for Blackpool went sadly awry and Special Force lost its stranglehold on the Railway Valley, Calvert's judgment about the White City proved to be only too true.

The West African brigade, with its three Nigerian battalions, which under Calvert had so wonderfully proved themselves in battle both as defenders of the block and as a component of his mobile striking force, had been prised away from his command and with the troops of Brodie's 14th Brigade - 2nd Bn. The Black Watch; 1st Bn. Bedfordshire and Hertfordshire Regt; 2nd Bn. York and Lancaster Regt. and 7th Bn. The Leicester Regt. - were now on the western flank of the Bumrawng Bum and were concentrating at the village of Nammun, about five miles to the south east of the great Indawgyi Lake and at the western end of the Kyunsalai Pass, which followed a long and torturous route over the mountains to the Railway Valley. A column of the Leicesters, under the old Chindit veteran, Geoffrey Lockett, pressing on remorselessly, secured the top of the pass on the 20th May, just 24 hours ahead of the Japanese, who were cut to pieces as they ran unsuspecting into Lockett's men. They withdrew leaving fifty bodies behind, but to take up a position astride the track leading to the Railway Valley and to offer increasing resistance to our men's advance down the track.

By this time Masters and 111 Brigade had already been in position at the block for a fortnight and under fierce pressure. It seems that our 14th Brigade and the 3rd West African Brigade did not look for an alternative route and were unaware of the much easier and shorter route further north from Mokso Sakan, which emerged from the mountains right at the site of Blackpool and which had been discovered by the scouts of 111 Brigade and then used by the brigade just a few days previously. The plan, which seemed on paper to be a good one, had been that the two brigades - then isolated on the far side of the mountains - should operate in the Railway Valley as a mobile striking force, in support of the defenders of Blackpool, so replicating the role which Calvert's mobile force had carried out so devastatingly and effectively at the White City. But the plan was already wildly adrift and the hapless defenders of Blackpool were to be left unaided to weather the full fury of the Japanese attackers, who had learnt some very important lessons and were now under a much more able and imaginative commander and were no longer being harried continuously and mercilessly, as they had been at The White City.

There were three elements in the timing of the establishment of the block at Blackpool, which were absolutely critical and were really self-evident. The new block had to be in place before The White City was abandoned, so as to replace one stranglehold on the Railway Valley by another; this had to be achieved before the heavy rains came in mid-May; and at or before the first steps were taken to establish the new block, the 3rd West African Brigade and 14 Brigade had to be in position and ready and able to deal with any enemy interference. The first two elements or conditions were fulfilled, but not the third, although the initial stages of the action at The White City had made it clear, beyond the shadow of a doubt, just how vital it was. The third condition could easily have been fulfilled had the two brigades gone straight up the Railway Valley and taken on the enemy garrison at Pinbaw and any other enemy forces in that area, instead of interposing between themselves and the achievement of that purpose, the massive obstacle of the Bumrawng Bum.

There may be a perfectly good reason why this was not done, but on the face of it, it does seem that Special Force H.Q. were not as closely involved as they should have been, in ensuring that these critical dispositions of the three brigades to an equally critical time scale, were carefully observed. Given more time, I should have liked to research the records at the Imperial War Museum and at the Public Records Office at Kew, to see what they disclose, but the deadline has defeated me. Maybe if I ever revise these notes, I shall get around to making this additional research. As one who was there, I should like to know, even if the exercise can now be nothing more than academic.

The location of the block at Blackpool had been determined from a consideration of air photographs and Masters had discarded the idea of approaching it via the Kyunsalai Pass, since this would have involved travelling several miles in the open up through the Railway Valley. He dropped off 30 Column of the 3rd/4th Gurkha Rifles at Mokso Sakan to establish a base and to maintain a picket of 100 men on top of the pass, and he then pressed on with the rest of the brigade over the pass, stopping on the 7th May on the banks of the Namkwin Chaung, a couple of miles short of the place where the new block was to be sited. Disguised as Burmese, he and his RAF officer, Squadron Leader "Chesty" Jennings, went forward by themselves to carry out a reconnaissance of the position and of the site for the airstrip. Late in the afternoon they returned and then led the brigade into its new position, though darkness had descended before this was completed. In the darkness, Dakotas came flying in with an urgent supply drop of wire, picks and shovels, which were speedily recovered and distributed.

With the morning light they were able to look around and take stock. They were on a cluster of small steep sided hills, densely covered with bamboo, rising abruptly, in places over 200 feet from the paddy fields below them. To their front and a mile away was the railway, with the road just beyond that and there, straight ahead, was Namkwin railway station, with, a couple of miles to the south, the village of Kyagyigon. They were at the confluence of two small rivers, the Namkwin Chaung, which flowed around the north east face of the block and its tributary the Namyung Chaung which came around the south and west of the position to join up with the Namkwin about 1,000 yards in front of them. From this eyrie there was an excellent view of the open countryside for miles in all directions, in a wide arc back so far as the line of the jungle covered hills they had just crossed. On the map the contours seemed to resemble the shape of an animal, lying face down, along a line roughly north east to south west, with its legs stretched out sideways.

Masters proceeded to identify the various features by using cricketing terms. The central spine, where brigade H.Q. was located, was "The Wicket", with "Keeper" to the west and "Bowler" and "Umpire" successively along the spine to the east. Beyond Umpire and half left from it was a very steep slope, almost devoid of vegetation, and at the bottom of it was a water-logged position carrying the sinister and topographically accurate name of "The Deep". From the top of the slope by Umpire and half right from the line of The Wicket, the ground rose abruptly to "Pavilion", which overlooked to the east the Namkwin Chaung and, on the far side of the Chaung, "Parachute Ridge". Proceeding clockwise from Pavilion was "Cover Point" followed by "Silly Point". To the north of the Wicket, in a clockwise direction were "Fine Leg", "Square Leg" and "Mid On". Everyone knew that whatever game was to be played on these rugged little hills in the next few days, it most certainly was not going to be cricket!

The day passed in a great flurry of digging and wiring, but their possession of the land had been so blatant and brazen that it was obvious from the start that the enemy would soon attack and they were not going to be able to produce a system of bunkers and strong points of the sort which was such a feature of The White City and Broadway. Not for Blackpool was there to be a position of rock-like impregnability on which successive waves of the enemy attacks would break in vain. There was a detachment of Japanese at Pinbaw, five miles north up the railway line and, in the absence of the main enemy force which was still engaged at The White City and would continue to be until 11th May when they discovered that the block had been abandoned, they attacked Blackpool night after night for five nights in a row.

The attacks, often by forces no larger than a platoon but pressed home with suicidal determination, came in against The Deep and the northern part of the perimeter manned by The King's Own, a good sturdy, north-country battalion, and the Cameronians. With concentrated mortar fire and long bursts on their water-cooled Vickers machine-guns, the defenders massacred the Japanese as they came on, fell back, regrouped and came on again and again with astonishing tenacity and lack of regard for casualties. But it was weary work, from which daylight brought no relief. Daylight meant unremitting, back-breaking labour in building the airstrip, humping supplies and trying to improve the defences.

The airstrip posed special difficulties. It was sited on the open
paddy fields between the point at which the two rivers met and
the steep hillside which formed the south facing side of the block.
Aircraft had to approach from the north east, but then had to land
on ground which was not level, but instead rose in a series of
stepped paddy fields surrounded by bunds. The cultivation of
rice involves flooding the paddy fields with water, the rice
seedlings being planted by hand in the flooded fields.
Consequently each individual paddy field has to be level and
surrounded by substantial mud walls, known as bunds, to contain
the water.   On rising ground this can only be achieved by
building the paddy fields in a series of level steps.   Removal of
the bunds themselves still left ground rising in a series of separate
levels and bumps, one of which, right at the north east or
approach end of the strip, was to prove to be a constant and
almost irremediable danger.

Furthermore, the airstrip was covered by dense scrub and it was
extremely difficult from the air to discern the flank boundaries of
the strip.   This made it fatally easy for an aircraft, as it landed,
to run off the strip to one side or the other.

A glider strip was the first priority to bring in bulldozers and
graders, which in turn would be used to improve the strip so that
it could receive Dakotas to bring in guns and troops.   Chesty
Jennings and his men worked without let-up in full view of the
Japs but were not attacked, and then the next day at about 7 am,
the first glider came in, under increasing light anti-aircraft fire
from the Japs. Just short of the strip and from a height of fifty
feet it banked and plunged straight into the ground. Three more
gliders followed and all crashed, two out of the four pilots being
killed.   They had succeeded in delivering a bulldozer, but the
grader had been smashed - and without this they could not finish
the strip.

Work continued all that day and into the night. Two Dakotas
arrived in response to the code word "Texas", but they then

realised that the strip was too short. The first attempted to land, bounced in the air and then with full throttle, was off again. The second landed and managed to pull up short. It was off loaded and took off, but no further planes could be received until the strip had been improved. The next night, the 13th May, the Dakotas came flying in, disgorging stores, jeeps and trailers, but one burst a tyre, shot off into the paddy and burst into flames, whilst a second was damaged and lay by the side of the strip, a third overshot and ended up in the paddy, where it was attacked and set on fire by a Japanese patrol. Amongst the loads were three 25-pounders (later a fourth came), six Bofors and six Hispano guns for anti-aircraft work. The 25-pounders were dug into position in a re-entrant on the steep slope above the airstrip and were soon in action against the enemy positions and against the road and railway and were able to prevent any movement on it by day. On one occasion they destroyed a complete train. The gunners' log records laconically - "Railway train engaged as pin point target by No.1 gun. Destroyed. 55 high explosive expended".

By now the enemy were moving up in force from the south and it was obvious that the brave but inept garrison at Pinbaw would shortly be avenged. Alarmed at what he saw, concerned at the non-appearance of the 3rd and 14th Brigades and disheartened that Lentaigne had not paid him a visit, Masters flew out by light plane to see Stilwell and Lentaigne, but got nothing to cheer him up. He was told that the other brigades were doing their best and that he could abandon Blackpool if his brigade was on the verge of destruction. It is, of course, easy to be wise after any event, but one would have expected Masters to have ensured that the other two brigades were disposed so as to be able to give him the immediate help which he knew full well it was essential he should have, and further, not to have moved into position unless and until that indispensable help was instantly available. It was rather pointless to cry after the event, when the die had been irretrievably cast.

The scene at Blackpool was reminiscent of Passchendaele, thick mud everywhere with trees blown to pieces and the revolting stench of putrefaction from the bodies of the enemy dead and other human remains hanging in the wire or lying around. The block was now under heavy artillery fire from 75mm guns and also from 105mm guns firing a shell of over double the weight and from heavy mortar fire. General Takeda, commanding the 53rd Japanese Division, was moving up to establish his H.Q. at Hopin, just south of the block, and prepared his plans to dislodge the enemy. After the death of Colonel Hyashi in his final abortive attack on the White City, General Takeda had taken over the operations at Mawlu, but did not discover that the block had been abandoned until 11th May, which was two days after it had occurred. News had then reached him of this new block at Namkwin and he had moved north to deal with it.

Night after night the enemy came in at The Deep, no longer in platoon strength, but in company strength and with set purpose. The King's Own kept holding and killing as one fanatical attack followed another, but our men were steadily tiring. On 17th May, their positions in The Deep were probed systematically by at least twelve pieces of Japanese heavy artillery and their second in command reported that there had been direct hits on his machine gun posts, killing their crews and he doubted whether they could hold another enemy attack. Masters relieved them with the Cameronians and as The King's Own passed him, they were walking like zombies, wild-eyed, their jaws sagging wide, obviously right at the end of their tether. The attack did not come in for another hour and the enemy waited until it was pitch black and torrential rain was falling. Time and time again they came against the positions in the Deep, but the fresh troops held, though it was four o'clock in the morning before the Cameronians could be sure that the last ferocious assault had been repulsed.

BLACKPOOL'S DEATH THROES

It was against this background that we marched across the paddy of the Railway Valley on the 19th May and arrived without incident at Blackpool, a heartening and greatly welcomed body of fresh troops. They could not immediately accommodate us within the perimeter and so we took up defensive positions for the night around the airstrip, with its clutter of crashed aircraft and with our backs against the well nigh precipitous slopes overlooked by Cover Point, Silly Point and Pimple. I found I had been appointed adjutant to take over from someone who had been filling the post temporarily since Scott Leathart had vacated the job to take over command of "D" company. The next day, the 20th May, we moved into the block to take over part of the perimeter and, to get the chronology into perspective, it was on that day that Geoffrey Lockett's column secured the top of the Kyunsalai Pass and also General Takeda completed the transfer of his Divisional H.Q. to Hopin. His move north had been greatly hampered by the fact that the Chindits had demolished six large bridges and much of the rolling stock had been destroyed. By using motor lorries equipped with flanged wheels they had managed to draw short trains, but all the freight had to be laboriously transported by hand around each of the breaks in the line.

Whereas the Japanese forces were now in a position to take fully organised and concerted action against Blackpool, the two brigades to whom we were desperately looking for support, were still on the far side of the Bumrawng Bum. There they faced a long hard struggle to force their way through the Pass before they would be even remotely in a position to help us, or even to pose any sort of threat at all to the Japs, who, in their attacks against us, were now to have it all their own way. They would be operating with fresh troops against those who, with the exception of the infusion of fresh blood which we had brought, were suffering from extreme fatigue, having had no proper rest for days on end. Our advent would allow patrolling against the enemy outside the wire to be strengthened, but it would still be by a comparative handful of exhausted men who, with all the fighting spirit in the world, could not hope to make any really effective impression against the strong forces now being ranged against us. The strong, wide ranging and most effective commando forces deployed at The White City, or their equivalent, were totally absent and we were to be left by our General, who had not even visited us, or the other two brigades, to sink or swim on our own.

What we saw, as we took up position within the perimeter, was chilling in the extreme. The morale of the men was at rock bottom - but who could blame them, after what they had been through - the place was pervaded by the overwhelming stench and sight of death, putrescent human remains and desolation; it was a sea of slippery mud churned up by shell and mortar fire and by traffic, and in places it was difficult to keep your footing. In The Deep, John Thorpe and "B" company took over from The Cameronians and Scott Leathart with "D" company took over in The Pavilion. As he did so, Scott came across a British soldier sitting in his slit trench and looking out over the valley. He took no notice as Scott jumped into his trench and asked what he was doing and then, when Scott tapped him on the shoulder, he rolled over sideways, stiff with rigor mortis. There was no obvious wound or other indication as to how he had come by his death, but what was equally chilling was that he should have been left there by his comrades or officers, who seemed not to have noticed or cared.

A platoon of "D" company under Jack Pasmore went to reinforce The Cameronians on Cover Point, Bill Smyly and a scratch platoon made up from H.Q. took over Silly Point, Reggie Twelvetrees and "A" company took over the rest of the perimeter overlooking the airstrip and Jimmy Blaker and "C" company went in alongside the Cameronians and King's Own on the northern part of the perimeter. These dispositions left the southern part of the perimeter overlooking the airstrip, the most lightly defended, since it was judged, wrongly as it turned out, that the enemy was least likely to attack from that quarter up the precipitous slope from the airstrip.

The area between the double Danert wire fence had been liberally sown with booby traps, leaving only two ways out clear of traps and this was a most undesirable state of affairs, hampering movement out of the block, as it did., The weapon pits we took over had little or poor head cover and our men set about finding timber to remedy this as best they could, but with free access to supplies outside the wire limited by the booby traps, this was far from easy. There was a heavy explosion on "C" company's front. Two riflemen trying to make their way through the wire had set off a "pineapple", killing one of them and badly wounding the other and I saw Jimmy Blaker at great personal risk, and with his characteristic courage and lack of concern for his personal safety, making his way through the field of booby traps to render them aid. He was sitting on the ground, with his feet tucked up under him, gingerly edging his way forward and carefully feeling in front of him as he did so. There were two main types of booby trap - the "pineapple", which was a large fragmentation bomb, looking very much like a pineapple, which was usually lashed into a tree at about waist height to achieve maximum effect and was actuated by an almost invisible black trip wire. The second type was a trap buried in the ground, into which was dropped a round of .303 ammunition, in an upright position. Pressure on the trap actuated a firing pin, which set off the round of ammunition, blowing off part of the foot, or entering the body from the ground upwards.

As previously mentioned, the contour map of the position looked rather like an animal, spread out and face down. An outlying hillock, known as "Pimple" and occupying the paw of the right hand hind leg of the "animal", that is at its south western extremity and overlooking the airstrip, was judged likely to be a fairly safe place and the H.Q. defence platoon and Burma Rifles were allotted its defence, but this feature was to be the first to be overrun by the enemy. Enemy activity steadily increased, the tempo of the artillery and mortar bombardment was raised, anti-aircraft guns were located to deal with our Dakotas and the probing at our wire grew and became much more skilful, no longer wild and reckless, but by troops who knew what they were doing. An attack came straight across the airstrip and although the Bofors guns depressed their barrels and had a field day, they were located outside the wire and at the last moment the crews had to abandon their guns and race back within the perimeter, in the nick of time. With the airstrip in enemy hands we no longer had any prospect of landing supplies by Dakota - any further supplies would have to be by the hit or miss method of airdrop, with the prospect of loads falling outside the very tight confines of our perimeter and with our aircraft much endangered by the greatly improved enemy anti-aircraft fire. Moreover, we could no longer fly out any of our wounded - a prospect which we viewed with profound dismay.

The rain poured down in a deluge and the place became even more of a hopeless quagmire. In the darkness, with all hell breaking loose, I had to make my way from battalion H.Q. on The Wicket, down the steep slope to "B" company, who were under fierce attack in The Deep. The telephone line to them had been cut and I had to find out how they were faring. They beat back the enemy and I offered to take back one of their men to the regimental aid post, near H.Q. He was on a stretcher and had been wounded in the abdomen by a grenade and had to be kept flat. We waded through the mud and water but, when we got to the slope, we were in trouble. It was as steep as the roof of a house and covered with a thick layer of mud which made it as slippery as polished glass, so we had to lie flat in the mud and try to push the stretcher up alongside us, but it was quite hopeless - we'd go up the slope a couple of yards and then slide all the way back, since there was nothing to hang on to. But I was determined not to be beaten, and after struggling for the best part of an hour we made it to the R.A.P., plastered with mud and thoroughly exhausted. I mention this to illustrate how difficult conditions were and to explain how Jack Pasmore was to get into a spot of bother later.

Supplies of food and ammunition ran desperately low and urgent messages were sent back to base for an airdrop, which was promised for the following day. No longer could airdrops be made by night since the extremely bad weather conditions made this quite impossible. We expected them to arrive in the morning, but it was 3pm before an escort of American Lightnings circled overhead - and then the Dakotas came. They came from the west, three of them, flying wing tip to wing tip, dipping down from the mountain range behind us, lumbering along slowly and holding a steady course at about fifty feet above our heads - and they kept steady on course with the Japanese opening up on them, with a frightening barrage of fire from their anti aircraft artillery, cannon and machine guns, the deafening roar of their engines matched by the thunder and yammering of the guns. They dropped a cloud of parachutes as they passed overhead. I'm not ashamed to admit that a lump came to my throat and tears to my eyes at this amazing display of sheer, cool, calculating heroism. And then one of them was hit and crashed to the ground in flames, as I gazed on in horror. Despite all their wonderful efforts to help us, many of the parachutes fell outside the perimeter and by the time everything had been collected and distributed, we had just one meal per man and ammunition for only another twenty four hours. We knew that there was just no possibility whatsoever of our receiving any more supplies.

Several days previously, whilst the Dakotas were flying in on a regular nightly basis, a new brigade major had arrived to take over the post vacated by Jack Masters. A tall, imperious figure in a floppy jungle version of a deerstalker hat, he was always known as "The Baron". He was always very much in evidence and went striding around, calmly and confidently issuing orders to all and sundry but not always,I fear, in a manner calculated to induce a ready and willing response. Though I never personally ran foul of him, I couldn't help thinking that as a "new boy" who had not borne the heat and burden of several weeks campaigning, as the rest of us had, a slightly lower profile would have served him better.

The artillery and mortar bombardment continued unabated and, just a few feet from me, a shell landed, cutting one of the men literally in two around his midriff and my nostrils were assailed, once again, with what I think is the most frightening battlefield smell of all - the stench of fresh human blood and guts. Nothing brings home to you with such fearsome realism, the immediacy of violent death and destruction. The stink of rotting corpses though revolting and horrifying, somehow belongs to the past, even if it's the recent past, and it lacks the savage, instantaneous impact of this, which physically assails your senses with a force like a hammer blow, and seems to flip your stomach over. The night of the 24th May was the very worst we'd experienced. All around the perimeter, the enemy came at us again and again remorselessly and relentlessly, taking all the devastating fire we poured at them and still coming back for more. We were taking heavy casualties, but their casualties must have been quite horrendous.

The first of our positions to fall to the enemy was Pimple, where the enemy then mounted machine-guns and a mortar observation post looking into our defences and from which they continually harassed the Cameronians. Sergeant Donald of the Cameronians took a platoon, charged up the slope, and in a magnificent effort, though he was wounded, wrested the feature from the enemy, killing about twenty-five of them. Shaking all over, he reported back to his C.O. with the classic comment - "I'm not a wee bit frightened, sir. I'm just trembling with excitement!" This exploit won the gallant sergeant the Distinguished Conduct Medal, but in the face of withering enemy fire the hill could not be held and the valorous platoon had to withdraw.

At first light on the 25th May, aided by a ground mist, the enemy attacked in great strength across the airstrip and overran our positions, ironically enough on the hill feature known as Silly Point. They also captured the 25-pounder gun position, but an attempt to take further ground was arrested by Bill Smyly who rallied his Gurkhas and countercharged hurling grenades. Colonel Walter Scott, D.S.O.,M.C. of the King's Regt., one of our bravest men and Colonel Thompson of the King's Own, also extremely brave, gathered together the two platoons, which formed our only reserves and I saw Walter looking up the hillside, steadily chewing gum, as he always seemed to do when he was in a tight spot, and then these two colonels personally led the two platoons in a desperate final effort to drive the enemy from Silly Point. But, despite the exceptional courage shown by all, the enemy could not be dislodged and Colonel Thompson was badly wounded in the shoulder.

BLACKPOOL ABANDONED.

The position was absolutely critical, with commanding positions irretrievably in the hands of the enemy and virtually no food or ammunition left, and at eight am. Masters had to make the decision which he had long feared but which was quite inevitable - to abandon the block and thereby save his brigade to fight another day, rather than to hang on and face annihilation in a "last man and last round" scenario.   The order was therefore given and to their astonishment the defenders found that, instead of having to fight their way out, there was a sector that the enemy had not guarded, at "B" company's position in The Deep, and that company went outside the wire to take up a covering position. All the heavy equipment had to be left behind - the guns, the mortars, the Vickers medium machine-guns and most of the mules.

One of the last people to be informed of the withdrawal was Jack Pasmore, on Cover Point. He and his men on that feature had done sterling work and had, so Alec thought, inflicted more damage on the Japs than any other platoon of ours. He had been wounded the previous evening, but had not reported the fact, choosing to stay bravely at his post. As he came away from the hill, he looked back and in the heavy mist, thought he saw some of his men on the hilltop and ran up the hillside calling to them. Only when he got virtually on top of them did he see that they were not Gurkhas - but Japanese! He "braked" hard, opened fire with his carbine, but his hat went over his eyes and he slipped up and went headlong, sprawling in the mud. I think this vaudeville act undoubtedly saved his life, because although the Japs opened fire on him, they were laughing so uproariously that they couldn't take proper aim and only "winged" him a couple of times, as he disappeared down the hillside a good deal faster than he had come up! Jack got his platoon back to "D" company before seeing the doctor, and then joined the walking wounded. He was awarded a well deserved Military Cross, I think for his splendid work with the platoon including the defence of Cover Point, rather than for the special display with which he left it!.

Those of the wounded who had any reasonable chance of survival, we took with us, and there were about sixty severely wounded, on stretchers or pony-back and a hundred walking wounded; anyone who could possibly hobble along just had to do so. But some were in extremis and were either already dying or very close to the end and would not be able to survive the long and hard haul over the mountains to Mokso Sakan. It was quite unthinkable that these should be left for the Japs, who would have slaughtered them brutally, either with the bayonet or sword, going out of their way to inflict the maximum suffering and humiliation. They were quite implacable, without a shred of compassion or humanity, and we knew of previous occasions, when they had overrun our hospitals, butchering staff and doctors as well as sick and wounded. What could not be avoided had to be done, and these desperately ill men were put out of their misery with a bullet, before the survivors left the Regimental Aid Post for the last time.

With battalion H.Q., I was, I think amongst the last to leave and, whatever lay ahead, it was a great relief to say goodbye to that veritable hell-hole. I found myself marching down a shallow jungle covered nullah and, to my left, and just below the height of my shoulder, the jungle gave way to a flat open clearing, perhaps a hundred yards or more wide, before on the far side, the jungle covered slopes took over once more. Across that clearing, right out in the open, many of our men were marching in extended order. I remember vaguely thinking that with the enemy all around us and so close at hand, since we had only just left the block, this was unwise and why had they not followed the usual infantry practice, so ingrained in you that you followed it instinctively, of making use of all available cover. Naturally, it was most important to make our escape as quickly as ever possible and to fan out as soon as we got through the gap in the wire, but this did not mean abandoning any available cover.

Suddenly all hell broke loose! In what was obviously a carefully coordinated operation, about four enemy machine-guns and a number of mortars simultaneously opened fire from the ridge behind us, bringing a devastating volume of fire down on the men who were crossing the clearing. In a trice, what had been a peaceful scene was turned into one of carnage, with several men hit and screaming and others lying still. About thirty yards out, right in the open, we recognised the portly form of our cipher sergeant, sprawled on the ground and writhing in pain. Alec, who was just in front of me, scrambled over the side of the nullah and I tagged along, hard on his heels to give a hand. The sergeant had been hit quite badly in the groin, but ignoring his repeated pleas to "leave me sir - I'm done for!", we each looped one of his arms around our necks and beat it in quick time, still under heavy fire, back to the shelter of the nullah, dragging him with us, but mercifully without being hit ourselves.

I was responsible for taking up a rearguard position with the defence platoon, so couldn't spend much time with the sergeant, but managed to organise a field dressing and for some of my men to construct a makeshift stretcher out of bamboo and a ground-sheet. The speed and skill with which they could fashion things out of bamboo, just with a kukhri had to be seen to be believed. I was not to see the sergeant again for some months, and then, back in India, I came face to face with him as he hobbled through the camp. He was glad we'd not taken him at his word and left him behind.

The brigade rendezvous was at a point marked "6R" on the one-inch map, about three miles up the Namkwin Chaung, which was now in spate, flowing fast and deep. The designation "6R" meant a difference in relative height of six feet and that the bank of the chaung, at that point, dropped six feet sheer, so it ought to be easy to locate. I looked around for a suitable spot for an ambush position and found one not far from the block, where the bank on the far side of the chaung rose steeply to the top of a small knoll about 150 feet high, at the foot of which it fell precipitously some fifty feet, straight into the fast flowing waters of the chaung. Despite their phenomenal skill at executing outflanking movements at great speed whenever they hit an obstruction, the enemy would find it difficult to outflank me on that side, though given time, they could do so. On my side of the chaung there was a patch of flat open ground which then gave way to a jungle covered slope and there was also jungle where we stood, facing back the way we'd just come. I'd have to watch my right flank. We carefully, swiftly and silently took up position in the jungle, selecting places which would give us the best possible fields of fire and all round protection.

Invisible and absolutely motionless in the jungle of which, in effect, we had become part, we waited tensely, looking to our front, all our senses keyed up like piano wires to catch the first indication of the approach of the enemy, weapons at the ready and grenades immediately to hand. There was no sound whatsoever, apart from the rushing water of the river and the incessant rain on the foliage above our heads, whence it cascaded on to our bodies. After all the fury and pandemonium of the last few days, it was difficult to get used to the stillness. We were very hungry, having had no food for the last couple of days and no prospect of any, since all that we'd had had been surrendered for the use of the wounded. We were cold, chilled through and through by the ceaseless rain, we were plastered head to foot in mud, we were dog-tired and utterly exhausted - but we were ALIVE and reasonably fit, when so many of our comrades were dead. We just wanted the chance to have a final crack at the enemy, before turning our backs forever on Blackpool - but that was not to be, since they did not follow us up.

Why they let us escape from the block, why they did not follow us up and harry us persistently in our sadly weakened condition, deprived of all our heavy weapons, as they must well have appreciated on looking over our old positions, we never knew. Louis Allen, with his special access to Japanese records and reminiscences, never offers an explanation. Perhaps General Takeda was heeding the old hunting admonition against following a wounded tiger into the jungle. Maybe he was glad to see us go and to have the opportunity to sit back and lick his wounds, of which we had administered plenty. Perhaps it was divine intervention and providence, as many believe. We had to give the columns, slowed down by all the wounded, ample opportunity to get away and into safe harbour for the night. After a couple of hours, which we thought would be adequate, we eased ourselves cautiously back into the jungle and followed where the others had gone, keenly alert to the possibility of an ambush, or a random encounter with the enemy.

We were quite on our own, there were no stragglers to pick up, but there was no mistaking the way the others had gone and after a few miles we left the chaung, taking a path, deep in churned up mud, which climbed steeply to our left in the direction of Nawku, nearly 2,000 feet above us. The brigade were in harbour not very far up this track and the battalion were acting as rearguard. As I linked up with them again, it was getting dark and Steve Smele kindly shared a mug of hot water with me. We had nothing else, but the warmth it gave was welcome. The rain was still falling incessantly and sitting upright, back to back, with half a blanket draped over our heads to try to induce some warmth, we dozed fitfully, longing for the dawn.

TO MOKSO SAKAN AND THE INDAWGYI VALLEY.

The next few days were purgatory. The march was really hard going, up and down steep slopes, through bamboo jungle thick enough to require laborious cutting in places and in almost continuous heavy rain. After three days we reached Gordon Upjohn's West African column at the top of the hill at 2,500 feet, just beyond Nawku, and they tenderly took over from our aching shoulders and starving bodies, the carriage of the seriously wounded. The battalion then went down the other side of the hill to Mokso Sakan, gratefully making use of the steps and other improvements to the track which they had made. At Mokso 30 column of 3rd/4th Gurkha Rifles had established a base, and we left the rest of the brigade on the hilltop trying with the aid of the West African column's radio to get in touch with Force H.Q., telling them to drop rations there and at Mokso Sakan.

We had now been without rations for five or six days and were literally starving. Our men employed their jungle lore to gather edible roots and bamboo shoots. We butchered one of our mules, but even in death the poor animal proved to be recalcitrant! Our teeth literally bounced off the meat, and we might just as well have been eating the sole of an old rubber boot. With a pressure cooker, which we did not have, and cooking for about 24 hours solidly, we might have made some impression but I, for one, didn't try it again. The men were quite horrified that we should even contemplate this and would have none of it, and I think they had a point.

When the much maligned "K" Rations did eventually float down to us from the sky, they were greeted with the enthusiasm usually reserved for manna from Heaven, or perhaps lobster thermidor! Not all our airdrops were free of sorrow. Some of the items came down "free-fall", that is without a parachute, and became exceptionally dangerous missiles. At Mokso, one of our men was hit by a sack of boots and killed instantly. At another place and time, I saw the redoubtable Lt.Col. Walter Scott, sitting peacefully on the ground, nearly hit by a free-falling box of ammunition, which crashed into the ground within two yards of where he was sitting. To have had such a brave and distinguished career ended so ignominiously, just does not bear thinking about.

Here, our men came into their own as experts in the building of shelters. In hardly any time at all, given just a good supply of bamboo and a kukhri, there appeared an individual shelter, with a sloping roof adequately thatched with bamboo leaves, and even a platform of split bamboo, a few inches above the soggy ground, on which you could sleep or rest, and any lashings required were also fashioned out of bamboo. I never ceased to marvel at the great skill they displayed as, in their casual, matter of fact way, two or three of them would get together, working in easy unison to make one shelter after another. But even a simple thing, such as the use of one of these shelters, was not to be without its own "occupational hazards". I well remember one night, when a mule broke loose, and in an act almost meriting capital punishment, started to eat the roof of the shelter occupied by Alec and me, when, of course, there were plenty of shelters around occupied by far less important people, which he could have eaten without causing us the least concern! Amusing now perhaps, but at the time, trying in the darkness and the rain, to round up a mule, loose both physically and morally, and to teach him the error of his ways, was not in the least amusing.

At Mokso Sakan we were just over four miles from the shore of a mighty lake - Indawgyi Lake, measuring fifteen miles long by five miles wide, at its widest point. There was plenty enough water coming down and it just had to go somewhere! Although a light plane strip was constructed at Mokso, the ground was low lying and much too waterlogged to take Dakotas. A brilliant idea was formulated of landing Sunderland flying boats on the lake to evacuate the sick and wounded and bring in supplies. Chesty Jennings, the brigade RAF officer, who knew a lot about these craft, was largely responsible for converting the idea into reality. He was able to send back to base technical details, which convinced them, in face of strong initial opposition, that the idea was feasible and indeed, should be tried out. Two old stalwart flying boats, which came to be known affectionately as "Gert" and "Daisy", were pressed into service and did sterling work. Their arrival was greeted by incredulity by our men, but caused a tremendous boost in morale.

The wounded in a very bad way and in great pain had lain on stretchers, under small makeshift shelters, with no real prospect of getting the advanced treatment which they needed, though our quite magnificent brigade medical officer, Doc. Whyte with his team and our regimental M.O.s laboured with a skill and dedication which was beyond praise. Now, the arrival of these great old aircraft made it possible for them to be flown back to hospital and they were ferried out to the Sunderlands by local sampans. Apart from those seriously wounded and the walking wounded, the British troops in general, who had been marching and fighting continuously since 7th March, were thoroughly exhausted and the casualty rate from malaria escalated. Altogether some 500 sick and wounded men were evacuated from Mokso Sakan.

We obtained new saddlery and new No.22 radio sets as well as some other heavy equipment - I think some Vickers machine-guns and 3 inch mortars, and rations and then on 3rd June we were sent north up the eastern side of the Indaw Valley, to block any enemy move down that side. A column of the Bedfordshire and Hertfordshire Regiment (never,never shorten the regiment's name to "Beds and Herts" - at least, not within their earshot!) from 14 Brigade was blocking the western side of the Valley. Under Stilwell, the Chinese 22 and 38 Divisions were moving south on Kamaing, which was almost due north up the Valley ahead of us, and we were to block the retreat on any enemy falling back before Stilwell's forces.

The Chinese were an odd lot. Sometime previously we had all been issued with bright orange coloured silk maps of our part of Burma and were given clear instructions that these were to be used as a recognition signal, as between the Chinese and ourselves. If we met a party of Chinese, we were to wave these brightly coloured silk maps, they would recognise us as friends and all would be well. One of our small patrols, who had been carefully briefed in this simple procedure, met a large party of Chinese, but a friendly wave of the orange coloured silk only drew a hail of bullets from the anything but friendly Chinese, wounding a couple of our men, who repaid the greeting by returning fire with much greater effect and, I think, killing four of the Chinese before beating a hasty retreat.

The track along the fringe of the valley was very low-lying and badly waterlogged, so that practically all the time we were wading through mud and water well above the top of our boots. To our right as we moved north, were the lower slopes of the hills, forming part of the range we had just crossed, and to our left, just beyond the narrow track and stretching away in the distance towards the lake, was a vast area densely covered by elephant grass, about ten feet high. If we moved off the track to the right and very slightly up the hillside, we sometimes caught glimpses of large herds of wild elephant in the distance, almost hidden in the elephant grass. Their presence gave rise to another unusual hazard. We would be moving along, slowly wading through the deep mud and water when suddenly, there would be a void, which we could not possibly have seen, below our leading foot, and we would go, face down, into the stinking muddy water and then have to drag ourselves and our sixty pounds of equipment, painfully to our feet once more. The elephants had been along the track before us! Imagine this experience inflicted, several times a day, on bodies which had already been stressed well beyond normal reasonable limits of endurance,and you'll be able to appreciate something of what we felt!

The mules, despite having four feet, didn't seem to appreciate it any more than we did. In spite of their stoutheartedness and surefootedness, they were often beaten by the mud. Under their heavy, awkward loads, they had great difficulty, even in the easier parts of the track and they would be floundering and splashing around, struggling hard to find and keep a footing. Then still struggling, or sometimes standing patiently still, they would sink right down in the mud, or just lie down in it in a state of complete exhaustion. There was then nothing for it but to unload the animal, transport the loads by hand to the drier ground at the side of the track, induce him somehow to free himself and lead him off the track and then replace the loads once more and have another shot. This sort of thing happened time and time again. Our progress was slow, painfully slow, and after a long really hard day, we subsided, totally exhausted, with little mileage to show for it.

Often our harbour for the night would be alongside a mountain torrent, cascading down the jungle clad slopes into the quagmire where we had struggled for most of the day. Under happier circumstances and without the almost incessant rain the locale might have been regarded even as exotically beautiful. I often took the opportunity of washing the mud out of my clothing and, since I did not have a change of clothing, of putting it back on again wet. This did not impose as much hardship as might appear because the choice was simply between being wet and muddy and being wet and clean.

I recall one day when our general discomfort was increased by an attack from hornets. I took a swipe at one which had just stung Alec on the side of his face and it rewarded me by stinging me between the eyes.   The poison it injected must have been of a particularly virulent kind, because Alec looked as if he had contracted an extremely bad attack of mumps and my face and eyes were so badly swollen that I could hardly see.   Needless to say it was also very painful, though not as bad as being stung by a scorpion, which has happened to me twice.

At first we were sent to Lakhren, 24 miles north, but were then recalled, back down the track again to Point 241, on the tip of a spur on the valley's edge and here we received two supply drops, which included two three inch mortars.   The Indaw Chaung flows out of the north eastern corner of the Indawgyi Lake which it drains into the Mogaung River, and about eight miles along the chaung, as the crow flies (many more miles if you measure it by the meandering course of the chaung) is the village of Chaungwa, where a standing patrol was established to prevent the Japs from using the chaung, and also to maintain contact with 14 Brigade on the other side of the lake.   Here Alec and Jimmy Blaker met a very old Gurkha woman who had been to Edinburgh for Queen Victoria's Jubilee, as ayah to an officer's family.   She was all agog because she'd had a dream of a hawk coming out of the west and chasing another hawk back to the east and was quite sure that this signified that we were going to drive the Japs out of Burma.   The standing patrol was also able to provide a most welcome addition to our diet in the shape of fresh fish.   The chaung was teeming with fresh fish, some very large indeed, as a hand grenade dropped into the water readily demonstrated.

On one occasion I took a small reconnaissance patrol of three men, from point 241 to link up with 14 Brigade and this was a difficult assignment, because of the elephant grass.   As soon as I got into it, I had great difficulty in finding my way.   The tracks through it were only about three feet wide and turned and twisted hither and thither, and the grass, towering about four feet above your head,   prevented any visual fixes, whilst the leaden sky completely obscured the sun. Working on a compass bearing also presented difficulties, since none of the tracks went on the desired bearing and even if they approximated to it, they did so for only a very brief distance and then went off at a tangent. If not extremely careful, it was easy to walk for hours and end up back where you started. I found that one solution was to set the general direction in which you had to go, and then when the track threw you off course, try to note by how far and in what direction and then to apply a correction when you came to the next junction of tracks. Much easier to state than to apply, but somehow it got me there and back. The elephants, making the tracks whilst foraging for food, couldn't care less about the direction you might want to follow. At the chaung we were lucky enough to find a canoe, which enabled us to cross easily and as we came into the shallows on the other side, we drove an enormous fish before us and one of my riflemen, showing great dexterity, whipped out his bayonet and speared it.

Capt. Geoffrey Jackson ("Jacko") took a patrol northwards up to Lakhren, which lay at the western flank of the mountain range, along the trail which we'd been following, and also to Manwe, which was a ferry point on the Indaw Chaung, to the north-west of Lakhren, and without disclosing his presence was able to discover the presence of Jap outposts at both places. Jacko was energetic, enterprising and fearless and we regarded him as one of our best patrol leaders. On 9th June, we got orders to occupy both Lakhren and Manwe, to stop any Japs moving south on that front and also to reconnoitre a track up to Padigataung, which was to the south east of Lakhren, and just over the crest of that part of the Bumrawng Bum. At about this time we heard the news of the "D" Day landings in Normandy, and also something which touched us more directly, the capture of Kamaing by the Chinese, under Stilwell.

Reaching Lakhren, we surprised the Japs and Jacko shot one of them but the rest dispersed in the jungle. "B" Company occupied Lakhren, whilst Scott Leathart and "D" company moved north west to Manwe on the banks of the Indaw Chaung. Just before first light they came upon the village, which had a single street lined on either side by houses and the plan was to attack with all three platoons, one to go straight up the street and the other two to go, one to the right and the other to the left to cut off the enemy escape routes. The right hand platoon bumped a party of the enemy and both opened up on each other simultaneously and the Japs made off into the jungle. Unfortunately Havildar Ran Bahadur was killed.

After investigating, Scott returned to the street and was conferring with the company subedar, Indra Bahadur, when a shot rang out and Scott was hit in the left arm. A Gurkha standing by, rushed the Jap sniper and shot and wounded him, and then finished him off with his kukhri. Scott had received a very bad wound to his left forearm and part of the ulna (the small bone) had been shattered and blown away. Subedar Indra Bahadur was bleeding from a chest wound and it turned out that this had been caused by a part of Scott's ulna, which had been driven by the impact of the sniper's bullet with such force as to be itself converted into a missile, which lodged between the subedar's ribs. Reggie Twelvetrees was following up with "A" company and took over to clear up the village, killing five Japs and dispersing the rest, who fled leaving their equipment and rations and a sketch map purporting to show their positions and ours.

Scott was transported back to H.Q. at New Lakhren, where our regimental M.O., Doc Wright carried out some first class initial surgery and other treatment, but some days elapsed before a light plane strip was constructed and Scott was flown out for full hospital treatment. It was a grievous loss to the battalion, to his brother officers and to his men. Scott had always been a great tower of strength to us all, a monument of quietly confident unflappability, than whom no-one was more reliable or steadfast, whose knowledge and love of the flora and fauna around us, which most of gazed on with unseeing eyes, was profound and served to garrison his heart and mind at times of stress. He had the wonderful knack of getting on the men's wavelength, possibly because of the close knowledge of the things of nature which they shared, to an extent which none of the others of us fully possessed. Mercifully he was not to be lost to us for ever, and after many months of operations and treatment, he rejoined us about 18 months later in Sourabaya, Java.

77 BRIGADE CAPTURES MOGAUNG.

Meanwhile to the north of the Railway Valley, the remnants of 77 Brigade were assaulting Mogaung from the south east. They were on the orders of the ruthless Stilwell, committed to a ferocious struggle, which they, who had suffered so much and for so long, ought never to have been required to undertake. But under the command of their indomitable leader Calvert, whose protests on their behalf had been in vain, they were, with the honour of their brigade and the Chindits at stake, making this final effort, to add to all that they had achieved at The White City and since then, this final page of glory, to include the winning of two Victoria Crosses by the 3rd/6th Gurkha Rifles. It was as if, as they faced the enemy, someone had shouted from their midst - "Show them your cap badges, lads!", and they were determined to do just that.

The attack on Mogaung presented exceptional difficulties. To the north it was bounded by the fast flowing Mogaung River and on the west by the Namyin Chaung now in spate. The country to the south and east was flooded and interspersed with lakes and marshes and the only access was along a narrow road, two miles long, running from the south-east and built up on a causeway above the floods. The attack had to go in on this extremely limited front - there was no other way, and flanking movements to either side were barred by a deep chaung bridged only where this road crossed it. The road was straddled along its length by a number of villages, each of which had been turned by the Japanese into a fortress, with bunkers constructed under the buildings and so sited that they could each give covering and supporting fire to the others.

Each position, extremely formidable in its own right, and garrisoned by fanatics, who only knew one way to fight, and that was to the death, had to be taken on and captured, before the wearisome and fearsomely costly process was repeated again and again. For fresh troops, in peak physical condition, it would be a daunting task, but the men who were being required to do the job, were literally burned out mentally and physically and had been taken time and time again to the limits of their endurance and beyond for a period of well over three months, without once being taken out of the line for rest and recuperation. The comparatively fresh Chinese troops, who were available on the northern·fringes of the town and who could have done so much to help, just refused to assist. Direct frontal attacks against heavily fortified enemy positions did not feature in their book at all. And the Chindits were therefore on their own, in a ferocious toe to toe slogging match.

It is, I fear, beyond the scope of this account, already a good deal longer than I had originally intended, to go into the battle in any detail, but I will just sketch the details of the actions in which the two Victoria Crosses were won, whilst having to admit that this is invidious, since so many acts of valour equally meritorious, have to be omitted. At the Pinh Mi Bridge, a rifle company of the 3rd/6th Gurkhas had been held up by fierce close range fire and their company officer Capt. Michael Allmand, in the first of three single-handed attacks, drove out the Japs with a shower of grenades hurled at close range and then, rushing in, killed three of the enemy with his kukhri, an extraordinary, if not positively unique feat for someone who was not a Gurkha. Stirred by this, his men cleared the bridge and the village, taking a position which had cost the brigade about 130 men killed and wounded. Two days later and further down the road, in front of the village of Natyigon, Michael Allmand was thirty yards ahead of his men, once again leading them into the attack, when they came under heavy machine-gun fire from the right hand end of the embankment nearest the bridge over the Mogaung River. Michael was in so much pain from trench foot that he could not run, but he splashed slowly through the mud and shell holes, and hurled grenades at the machine-gun post, until he had silenced it, but was mortally wounded as a result.

In the same action, "B" company of the 3rd/6th Gurkha Rifles were attacking the bridge itself and were pinned down by fire from a strong point and the leading section was reduced to three men. These three got up and charged the strong point, but two of them were shot down, leaving only Rifleman Tul Bahadur Pun standing. He charged the strong point alone, firing his Bren gun from the hip, killing three Japanese and putting the rest to flight, then from that position, he gave his comrades supporting fire as they fought their way to take the objective. Both these men were awarded the Victoria Cross, made not of gold or any other precious metal, but just of gun metal, inscribed with two simple words - "For Valour" - but could any two words, in that context, possibly be more eloquent.

Towards the end of the battle, the Chinese became involved and played a minor part, still refusing to engage in any coordinated attack on a heavily defended position. They were full of praise and admiration for what 77 Brigade had done, but added that they could have achieved the same with far fewer casualties, by going about it much more slowly and behind much heavier artillery strikes. The Chinese attitude must have been due entirely to leadership, because within a very few years, under different leadership - Communist - the chief characteristic of their troops in Korea was that they came on and on against their opponents, like great waves of the sea, without any apparent regard for the fearsome casualties they suffered. Despite the achievements of 77 Brigade, which must be unsurpassed in the history of infantry endeavour, Stilwell still refused to give them credit and the news put out by his H.Q. was that the Chinese had taken Mogaung, with the assistance of the Chindits. When Calvert picked up the news broadcast, he sent his famous signal to Stilwell's H.Q. -

"The Chinese having taken Mogaung 77 Brigade is proceeding to take Umbrage".

Not long afterwards Stilwell and Calvert met face to face and Stilwell commented -"You sent some very strong signals." Calvert, who was accompanied by Lentaigne, had been urged to keep his unruly tongue under control but, unabashed, he replied - "You should have seen the ones my brigade major wouldn't let me send!." This struck exactly the right note and opened the way for Calvert to give a factual account of the operations of his brigade and details of the casualties they had suffered. Stilwell seemed, or affected, to be unaware of this and indicated that his staff was to blame. However, it is difficult to avoid the conclusion that the problems, in fact, arose from his own personal deeply rooted antipathy to the British since his subsequent actions indicated no real understanding or appreciation of what our men had done.

FROM LAKHREN UP INTO THE HILLS.

On our own front there followed a period of intensive patrolling, when we were often clashing with the enemy. "A" and "B" companies went well forward up the valley to deal with the enemy who were being forced southwards by the Chinese pressure in the north east, killing many of them whilst the rest dispersed into the jungle. These parties of the enemy were completely isolated in nearly uninhabited and quite inhospitable jungle and many must have starved to death, as they tried to get away. "C" company had located a track up into the hills to Padigataung, which they occupied after driving out a Japanese post and capturing a machine-gun, and they had also improved the track. The brigade followed them up the hill but the battalion remained, for the time being, at Lakhren, to make contact with the Chinese and to assist in the evacuation of sick and wounded. The flying boats had gone out of service, but had been replaced by a flotilla of small boats and rafts, floating down the Indaw Chaung to Kamaing, and some rubber assault boats had also been brought down to operate in bringing up casualties from the Indawgyi Lake. I believe this service was run by our former engineer, Leigh-Mallory.

Meanwhile 14 Brigade had forced their way through the Kyunsalai Pass and the 3rd West African Brigade, using our old pass from Mokso Sakan had emerged quite close to Blackpool and both brigades were operating in the Railway Valley and north of it. After the fall successively of first Kamaing and then Mogaung, where the once elite Japanese 18th Division had lost the whole of its 128 Regiment, the survivors fell back to fortify the small towns of Sahmaw and Taungni and during the early part of August, the capture of these two towns was to be the last battles in which the Chindits were to engage. Well over to the east Morrisforce, after operating with notable success against the Bhamo-Myitkyina Road, were employed in the final assault on Myitkyina.

From Padigataung the brigade now began pushing columns down the eastern slopes of the mountain range to raid enemy dumps between the lower slopes and the road, leading up towards Mogaung. The British battalions, some well below half strength, were re-organised. The King's formed one column under Col. Scott and the King's Own and The Cameronians combined together to form one weak battalion under Col. Henning. These British forces, together with 30 Column of 3rd/4th Gurkha Rifles, who had not been at Blackpool and were almost full strength, forced their way down the eastern flank of the mountains back into the Railway Valley, where our patrols were constantly clashing with small groups of the enemy. One of these patrol actions resulted in the death of a vibrant and gallant character, Capt. Mike McGillicuddy of 30 Column. A member of the Irish gentry, he had joined in the ranks, where he had won the Military Medal and then, for gallantry at Pinlebu, he had won the Military Cross and his loss was keenly felt.

As a final effort, we were ordered to operate against the road and railway in the vicinity of Taungni and the battalion therefore moved to Padigatawng. The Cameronians, now reduced to only 50 rifles and quite incapable of engaging in any further attack, made their way back to Lakhren, which we'd recently left, to relieve our "A" company, who were then moving to join us. As we moved forward from Padigatawng, we left there the King's Own, who were now also sadly depleted.

Amongst the British troops, men were dying other than from a diagnosed illness and it must have been about this time that, puzzled, I asked Doc. Whyte the reason for this. He told me that the men had suffered so much and for so long, that some of them quite simply had just lost the will to live. Doc. Whyte was our brigade medical officer, a truly remarkable man whose devotion to the men under his care was beyond all praise and was recognised by the award of the D.S.O. The will to survive must surely be one of the most, if not, in fact, the most fundamental and compelling of all the drives in the human personality. Any normal man will do almost anything just to survive, just to keep on living. How fearful therefore must be the pressures brought to bear on the human spirit, to make it relinquish the will to live and instead just to lie down and die. Yet these were, in fact, the immense pressures which over the last four months and more, had been brought to bear on us. I found it a very sobering, indeed frightening thought that some men, having survived the assault of wounds and disease had yet succumbed to the psychological assault and, what is more, had done so when relief was almost in sight.

THE APPROACH TO POINT 2171.

Ahead of us the narrow precipitous track passed over the crest of the mountains at a hill feature marked on the Ordnance Survey map as "2171", which meant quite simply that this was its altitude above sea level, measured in feet. It was destined to become known and ever remembered as "Point 2171" and as such to win a place of undying fame in our regimental history. In the vanguard of the marching columns were the Gurkhas of 30 Column (3rd/4th Gurkha Rifles) and just before dark on the evening of 6th July they bumped and cleared the enemy from a small village and clearing, on the western slopes of Point 2171. The following morning, with three inch mortar support, they pushed further up the trail, clearing an enemy outpost and killing five or six of them. The brigade established itself around the clearing and took the first of a number of very successful airdrops.

Whilst here we often came under shellfire from an enemy 75mm at Hkamutyang about three or four miles away to the north. Being under shellfire is not normally an amusing experience, but on one occasion it was, because of the percentage of misfires. I'm not sure whether this was caused by dud ammunition or just by the angle at which the shell hit the ground. You could hear the bang from the distance as the gun was fired followed by the low whistle of the shell overhead and then a sort of heavy splashing sound as the shell hit the ground and ploughed its way through the mud and water, but without exploding. This happened so frequently that I formed the mental picture, to me an amusing one, of a rather pained looking group of Jap gunners, with heads cocked on one side, listening for the sound of the explosion which never came.

The men of 30 Column had forced the enemy back up the hillside and the plan was that our battalion would capture the hilltop early in the morning of the 9th July. Under command of John

Thorpe, "B" company would attack up the existing trail and "C" company, led by Jimmy Blaker, would carry out a left flanking movement and come in against the enemy's flank, putting in the attack from north to south. At the request of "B" company, to which "C" company agreed and Alec acceded, there was to be no covering fire, because the density of the jungle made it extremely difficult to pinpoint the enemy position, and also there was no radio with which to control the covering fire.

I was to take out a recce patrol, just before first light, and make my way up the trail ahead of "B" company to check that it was clear of any enemy and thus give "B" company a flying start. I went along to confer with Jimmy and to see if he had any special orders for me. It was dark and he was in one of the native huts on the edge of the clearing, eating his evening meal of the usual hash from his mess tin, by the light of an electric torch, which he'd taken from the enemy in one of his brushes with them. It was an unusual sort of torch, operated not by a battery but by a dynamo, driven by a lever on the side of the torch. Jimmy held it in the palm of his left hand and as he squeezed the lever with his fingers, the little dynamo inside the torch gave him light for a few seconds at a time.

We had heard of the progress of our invasion of Normandy, that the beach-heads had been firmly established and there was a feeling of optimism abroad. It seemed certain that the war in Europe would soon be over, and that with all the war effort re-directed to the Far East, perhaps it would not be so long before our war would also be at an end. The enemy push on Imphal and Kohima had not succeeded and it looked as if we had at last got the enemy on the run. We were not to know this, but in fact Mutaguchi would on the next day, the 9th July, the very day of our attack on Point 2171, be giving to his divisions the order to retreat from the Imphal and Kohima fronts. Jimmy and I fell to talking about what we would both be doing after the war was over. He was planning to qualify as a doctor and I was intending to go back to the study of law and to qualify as a solicitor. Tomorrow might well be a tough assignment, but we didn't harp on it. After all, tomorrow was another day.

Jimmy, like most of us was not a regular soldier, but held an emergency commission and had come to us from the famous Scots regiment, The Highland Light Infantry, sometimes rather disrespectfully called "Hell's Last Issue". He was far from being the archetypal tough guy. He was only about five feet nine inches tall and slender in build, but there was a glint in his eyes and a determined set to his jaw and mouth, which made you realise that there was plenty of hidden toughness and sheer ruthlessness built into that lightly constructed frame. Come to that of course, none of our men were set in the "A.T.G. style". They were short, mostly around five foot three or four inches tall and slightly built, but were regular little balls of fire. Jimmy was an expert with our infantry company weapons, carbine, rifle, tommy gun, machine-gun, pistol, grenade and kukhri and indeed, in the scrimmage at Taung Bazaar, he had personally killed, I think seven out of the sixteen Japs who had died. His future purpose was to bring healing and help to mankind as a doctor, but his present purpose was to do quite the reverse to any Japs he came across, and to do that as efficiently and speedily as possible. As a modest, self-effacing person, he would be quite horrified to have his activities put in this way, but in fact, this is what they amounted to. To this end, he was far more serious about his soldiering than most of the others of us were.

He never relaxed or let up in the training of his men and, though I'm sure he would never have put it in this crude way, his object was to hone his rifle company into the most efficient killing machine possible. In the context of what I've just stated, he would have ruled out the word "killing", as being obnoxious, but in the light of the way he operated, the addition of the word was justified. He would, I'm sure have wanted to turn the idea around and point out that efficiency would minimise the casualties suffered by his men in their encounters with the enemy. All very true of course, but it was not his style on meeting the enemy, to be concerned about limiting his own casualties, but to inflict the maximum on the enemy. His tactics were to go in, and to go in hard. Although he did not so express it, he was very much a believer in the old adage - "Whatsoever thy hand findeth to do, do it with all thy might!"

To go out with his rifle company on patrol was an object lesson in how it should be   done. The company moved swiftly, stealthily and in complete silence, from one bound to another, one platoon dropping down into position almost automatically to cover the advance of the others - and all without a word of command, or almost without a word of command - working, where visibility permitted, almost entirely from his hand signals, like an enormous well oiled machine. It was as if he were the conductor of a big symphony orchestra, with the eyes of all his men closely watching his hands as he worked from a score which would bring not delight to those he met, but death. His men looked to him for everything and trusted him implicitly, in an attitude which was almost reverential, and he, for his part, was zealous to ensure that their confidence in him would never be misplaced.

He was not one of the most light hearted members of the Mess, his zeal and great enthusiasm for soldiering and the training of his men tended to make him rather serious and reserved, but he was never self opinionated or pompous or a bore, but was very popular with us all because we all recognised his exceptional qualities and some saw in him the soldier which they would like to be, even if they did not express it in those terms. He was just the sort of man to have around when you were in a tight spot, and no infantry officer can say more, or ask more, of one of his brethren than that.

POINT 2171 CAPTURED AND HELD.

The morning was dry, but dank and heavily overcast and as I pressed cautiously up the trail with my men, I rounded a bend and there, indistinct in the half light was something which made me duck into the undergrowth. There on the trail ahead of me, was a Japanese machine-gun on its tripod and squatting upright, on his heels behind it, and in the firing position, was a Jap. I did a sort of double take and then realised that the man was quite dead. He must have died instantaneously and he was frozen in death in the exact posture he had adopted at the instant of death, save that his chin was on his chest and his hands hung loosely by his side. He must have been killed by 30 Column, and I left him as he was, to give someone else a fright.

Jimmy Blaker and his men would have to carry out a difficult manoeuvre, in making a wide swinging movement, out to the left, through virgin jungle and so would take longer to reach the objective than John Thorpe and "B" company. The plan therefore was that, so as to ensure that both company attacks went in simultaneously, John would take his timing from Jimmy. John would get as close to the enemy as possible, wait till he heard firing on Jimmy's front and then go in with his own men. Looking back on it, it seems to me that my patrol might have been, in this light, somewhat counter productive. It did enable "B" company to move up the trail faster than they might otherwise have done and in consequence they bumped the enemy before Jimmy did.

I was very fond of "B" company. My very first job with the battalion, when I joined it, was as company officer to "B" company, and I got to know the men well - I'm sure I'd have felt exactly the same about any other company in the battalion, if I'd served with them.   There was Jemedar Kesh Bahadur, a real ebullient fire eater, with a very keen sense of humour, who had been a platoon havildar (sergeant) when I joined the company and held the Indian Distinguished Service Medal (the equivalent of the British D.C.M.) and who was to win the Military Cross before the day was out.   There was Jemedar Yem Bahadur, another tremendous leader, and the third platoon commander (at least, he was when I was with the company) was Jemedar Kehar Singh - a more miserable, sad and severe looking man you could scarcely expect to see and yet his character was the complete opposite.   To my mind he was the exact Gurkha counterpart of the famous American comic, Buster Keaton, to whom he bore a striking facial resemblance and he was a great favourite with his men. Without changing his sour and miserable facial expression in the slightest, he would mutter something out of the corner of his mouth and all his men within earshot would collapse, roaring with laughter.

Making their way cautiously up the trail, "B" company came to an extremely difficult section, with a gradient of 1 in 2 on slippery clay, through dense jungle, full of vines and creepers, which they had to negotiate, literally on hands and knees. At that extremely awkward moment, they met a veritable storm of medium machine-gun, light machine-gun and rifle fire at a range of only about 20 yards, which was sweeping the entire company from front to rear. They therefore went straight into the attack then and there - in truth there was no real alternative - with Jemedar Kesh Bahadur and 10 platoon on the right and Jemedar Yem Bahadur and 11 platoon on the left.

But it was not a case of a quick dash for a few split seconds, to bring them right into close quarters amongst the enemy. The best pace that could be made on that death dealing slope was a slow scramble - and that had to be made in the face of the most murderous fire imaginable. When I got to the hilltop much later, I felt a chill clutch at my heart as I saw that all the trees and saplings surrounding the enemy machine gun pits had quite literally been chopped down by the machine-gun fire, leaving ragged stumps behind, and there were great mounds of empty cartridge cases and metal strips which had been fed into the enemy machine-guns (their guns were strip-fed, not belt-fed, like our Vickers). Yet these gallant and great-hearted men did not flinch, they pressed on and in a display of courage, which could not possibly be exceeded anywhere, they took the front edge of the enemy position, at the cost of twenty three men, including the company commander and Jemedar Yem Bahadur. Alec, who is not given to hyperbole, states soberly in his notes - "I do not believe anything could exceed the courage shown by those platoons that morning." The award of decorations, though not an exact measure of gallantry, since many actions of extreme bravery go without official recognition, is some indication, particularly in a battalion like ours, where decorations were bestowed only for exceptional merit. This action resulted in the award of one Indian Order of Merit, one Military Cross, one Indian Distinguished Service Medal and four Military Medals, all to "B" company.

John Thorpe was wounded in the knee by a grenade splinter and also by a bullet, which creased the back of his neck, but he stayed on for the time being. Jemedar Yem Bahadur was very severely wounded and had his right femur shattered just above the knee, by a burst of machine-gun fire. He was brought down the hillside on a stretcher, wallowing in a pool of his own blood, and when at his command, the stretcher bearers came to a halt, so that he could make his report to the colonel, they did so clumsily and abruptly and I saw some of the blood sluice out of the leading edge of the stretcher and cascade on to the ground. He was in agony, his shirt soaked with sweat and great rivulets of sweat pouring from his face and yet amazingly, he had lost none of his fighting spirit. He was not in the least concerned about his wound, only that he had been cut down before he could get to grips with the enemy. He insisted on making a full report on the situation to Alec, and finished by practically ordering him to continue the attack. He was then carted off, still protesting at not having been able to get in amongst the Japs with his kukhri!

Alec ordered "B" company to hold their ground until the arrival of "C" company, when they should both be able to go in together and finish the job. They remained, exchanging fire with the Japs at twenty yards range.

Meanwhile "C" company had slogged their way for a mile and a half, through jungle so dense that they had to cut their way through some of it. Clambering downhill, they dropped about 600 feet, followed by an ascent of some 1700 feet, through the most intricate mess of re-entrants and gullies, in which they could easily have got hopelessly lost, had it not been for Jimmy's first class map reading. They arrived on the enemy's north flank about half-an-hour after "B" company had first bumped the enemy, and immediately encountered the same devastating storm of machine-gun fire. They were in danger of being pinned down, and Jimmy made his way forward. He appreciated right away that the main volume of fire was coming from a medium machine-gun just fifteen yards away flanked by light machine-guns and, that since it was so close, he had no room for carrying out any manoeuvre.

There was nothing for it but to go straight in, and to go in hard. And, if this were not carried out immediately, his men would suffer heavy casualties. Jimmy was never one to get any of his men to take any risk which he personally was not prepared to take, nor was he prepared to allow his men to suffer casualties which prompt action could avoid. In an act so characteristic of this singularly brave and stout-hearted man, he scrambled to his feet and cheering his men on, rushed straight at the medium machine-gun firing his carbine, regardless of the fearsome storm of fire coming from the enemy. On many an occasion in the past, this great dash and elan had carried him through, to live and to fight another day, but sadly, this was not to happen today.

Before he reached his objective, a burst of machine-gun fire struck him in the midriff. The impact stopped him dead in his tracks and flung him staggering backwards against a tree. He had been hit badly. and as his legs buckled underneath him, he slowly sank to the ground, his back still against the tree trunk, all the while cheering his men on as, inspired by his selfless leadership, they charged past him to capture the hilltop.

His second-in-command, Capt. Jimmy Sweetman, knelt by his company commander to see what he could do to help, but a quick look at the wounds was enough to convince him that nothing could be done, and Jimmy's life was fast ebbing away. He had himself had a very narrow escape. There was a bullet hole through the crown of his hat. An inch lower and he would also have been amongst the dead. Though mortally wounded, Jimmy's thoughts and concern were not for himself, but for the safety and security of his men, and that the gain they had made should be consolidated against the enemy counter-attack, which would almost certainly be coming in shortly. He therefore told Jimmy Sweetman to go out to their right flank and check that they had linked up with "B" company. Sweetman hesitated, indicating that he wanted to stay with his old friend, to render what help and comfort he could. Of course, it would have been a great comfort for Jimmy to have had his friend and trusted comrade by his side, during these last few minutes of his life, but, a soldier not just whilst he was on his feet but to the very end, he put his men, his company and his regiment before himself and said to Sweetman, quite firmly, if not brusquely:- "That's an order!" With a heavy heart, Jimmy Sweetman turned away from his friend, never to see him again, to carry out this, his last order and to link up with "B" company, so as to secure the hilltop against the enemy. I do not think these details have been published before, but they are as related to me by Jimmy Sweetman just after the event, though the words are mine.

The enemy was soon counter-attacking and contesting the occupation of the hilltop, and in the confusion, there was no opportunity to afford Jimmy's body a burial, and he was dragged away into the jungle and covered with leaves. Months later, Capt. Noel Shead of our battalion, on a temporary assignment to the War Graves Commission, to locate the bodies of our men and give them a proper burial, returned to Point 2171 and after a lengthy search, came across Jimmy's skeleton, identified by his "dog-tag", with a thirty foot bamboo growing through the pelvis. These specially treasured remains were carefully gathered and interred in the Sahmaw Chaung War Cemetery.

Most of us, on at least one occasion during the year, stand in silent tribute as Laurence Binyon's remarkably evocative words are recited in our hearing :-

> "They shall grow not old, as we who are left grow old,
> Age shall not weary them, nor the years condemn,
> At the going down of the sun, and in the morning,
> We will remember them."

As I bow my head and close my eyes, there comes floating into the memory, half shrouded by the mists of nearly half a century, a vision of my old comrades of long ago, who gave their all, or maybe had that taken away from them, irrespective of their personal preferences. Frozen in time, they have a well remembered smile on their faces, their backs are straight and upright, they have a spring in their steps, they are keen and alert, so very different from what we now are, but once were then. I see Jimmy coming to report to the colonel, or to receive orders for some foray against the enemy and snapping smartly to attention and giving that oh, so well remembered salute. It was a salute which would have made any self respecting drill sergeant cringe. As his hand came up, his elbow was so far forward that the tip of his thumb well-nigh touched the tip of his nose. But I wouldn't want to change it in the slightest, even if I could. It was his military signature. He went into action thumbing his nose at all the dangers, and he paid the ultimate price and did, in truth, give his all.

The news and the manner of his death as it came back to us rocked us on our heels, and made the victory bitter-sweet. But one thing was certain - a citation for the supreme award for valour was amply justified. Alec roughed out the draft of the citation and I got it into shape and fair copied it in pencil on the back of a sheet of paper torn from a message pad. It was couched in the usual flat, matter of fact military prose, but it was a citation for the Victoria Cross. It was signed by Alec and then passed to brigade, where the brigade commander added just one word - "Recommended" and signed it, then accompanied by the written statements of three witnesses, it went back to base H.Q.

Some years later I tried to recover that small scrap of paper, in itself so insignificant, yet so redolent of the history of the battalion, that I thought it would be prized by the Gurkha Museum. But it was not to be. Some weeks later I received a most apologetic letter from Army Records, expressing regrets that this with other records had been destroyed. The enquiry must have caused them concern, since the letter was signed by a Lieutenant General. The original records may have gone, but the memory will live on for a few more years in the minds and hearts of the rapidly dwindling band of those of us who were there. Away in India, at the Regimental Centre, the reflection of that memory is kept alive in naming the 3rd battalion - "The Chindits" and one of their roads "Blaker" and also with a day of special celebration on the 9th July each year to mark the anniversary of the action.

I have digressed, but for us at that time, there was to be no digression since the hilltop had to be held against repeated enemy counter-attacks. Climbing up the almost impossible track to the top, part of the way virtually on our hands and knees, it was so steep and difficult, I was greatly saddened to come upon the bodies of the men who had died, lying just where they had fallen, with their faces towards the foe. Where possible, with the limited time available, we buried them where they lay, in the nearest available weapon pit, without ceremony, save to take off their boots, so as to remove the contamination offered by leather to any devout Hindu.

They were men of "B" company, whom I knew and remembered well, and I had a strange experience. Back in camp in India, the men's favourite pastime had been the game of volley-ball, to which in their very simple and totally unsophisticated way, they brought a zest and enthusiasm and a boundless energy, both as players and spectators, which it was captivating to behold. To see such joy and pleasure created by a very simple net and ball was a great tonic and the visual images rivetted themselves in my mind. Now, as not far short from tears, I gazed sadly at these pitiful crumpled forms at my feet, my memory played an odd trick and in a mental flash-back, I saw and recognised them again, individually and clearly, in the very act of taking part, some as well known protagonists and others as spectators, in those volley-ball matches of long ago. It was as if my senses were not prepared to accept the evidence of my eyes, but wanted to overlay each sad motionless body with a happy image of him culled from memory. It just did not seem possible that all that boundless zest and over flowing joy of living, could, within the space of a few horrifying minutes, have been so cruelly extinguished for ever. Yet this was the sad, desperate reality of what had happened. Following the strict Gurkha code - "Kaphar hunnu bhanda marnu ramro" - (It is better to die than be a coward) - they had gone unflinching and unyielding to their deaths. I turned away with a sad and heavy heart.

Noel Shead, John Thorpe's second-in-command, took over command of "B" company and Michael Bates assumed command of "C" company. We held Point 2171 for two separate spells. Following the attack which won the hilltop, we stayed there until 11th July, when we were relieved by The Kings and 30 Column. Then we took over from them and held the hill again from the 15th to the 17th July. During those periods we were frequently under attack and the enemy were obviously desperately keen to repossess the hill. To the east, just beyond Point 2171, the reverse slope of the hills fell away sharply to the Railway Valley, with the village of Taungni and the road and rail quite close at hand. They were determined to prevent us at all costs, from blocking the road and rail yet again.

Their attacks followed the same pattern each time. They had several 81 mm mortars, two 75 mm guns and one 105 mm gun, which were sufficient to make things very uncomfortable for us and to add to the casualties we had already suffered. There would be a heavy artillery and mortar bombardment, under which they would press home their attacks against our wire under cover of heavy machine-gun and rifle fire. This would go on for about half-an-hour, then there would be a break for about five or ten minutes, then they'd attack again for another five of ten minutes, under cover of which they removed their dead and wounded, of which I'm sure there were plenty. Despite all their efforts, they never managed to penetrate our defences, yet they just would not give up, but came back again and again for more punishment.

A couple of our Vickers medium machine-guns were sited, one on either flank, to lay down a belt of fire across our front, to catch the enemy in enfilade as they came up the steep slope to our wire, and these were particularly effective. On one occasion, right in the middle of an attack, one of the machine-gunners came rushing up to me to say that his gun, which was on our left flank, had jammed and couldn't be cleared. I hopped out of my foxhole, scooped up a spare Vickers complete with tripod, in my arms, and rushed through a hail of mortar, artillery and machine-gun fire to get it into action to replace the defective one. It was an awkward and very heavy load, I think well over one and a half hundred-weights, and nowadays I don't suppose I could even lift the tripod by itself.

At the foot of the hill, just to the north of the clearing, was our mortar platoon, dug into position on the top of a ridge in the middle of a plot of Indian corn, which was now almost ripe. Some of us, when we were down at the foot of the hill, away from Point 2171, resorted to the platoon post to sample the Indian corn, which was delicious, as much as to confer with our mortar officer, John Bradburne. The platoon did not have any additional infantry protection, but had to fend for itself as well as operate the mortars. Northwards from the position, there was a wide valley and on the other side of the valley, a ridge where we often saw the enemy moving around. This was Hkamutyang, and was a frequent target for the mortars. On occasions, the mortar platoon came under direct attack from enemy infantry and once a grenade landed in one of the mortar pits and exploded but without injuring any of the three men in the mortar crew.

The platoon havildar, Tirtha Bahadur, won the Military Medal for controlling the mortar fire whilst under attack and for ruthlessly hunting down the enemy who had attacked the position. John Bradburne was equally courageous. He had been posted out to our 2nd battalion in Malaya and joined them on 23rd December 1941, just 15 days after the Japs had landed at Kota Bahru. It is not generally appreciated that the enemy landings at Khota Bahru at 0015 hours local time (0215 hours Tokyo time) on 8th December 1941 took place 70 minutes before the attack on Pearl Harbour, which was at 0325 hours Tokyo time, so it was these landings, not the attack on Pearl Harbour which marked the treacherous entry of Japan into the War, prior to any formal declaration of hostilities. The first wave of the assault troops came from the elite Japanese 18th ("Chrysanthemum") Division, mentioned earlier in this account as involved in the attack on Imphal. The invasion fleet had been spotted a few hours earlier by a Sunderland flying boat and the landings were strongly opposed by the small band of defenders, the 3rd Battalion of 17th Dogra Regiment, Indian Army.   They and the   shorebased artillery batteries gave a good account of themselves and managed to inflict one third losses on the invaders and to sink two Japanese troopships before they were overwhelmed.

John was involved with the battalion in some heavy fighting as they carried the brunt of the rearguard actions on the road south from Alor Star.   Then on 8th January 1942 in the fearful disaster at Slim River, they lost 5 officers and 500 men comprising three rifle companies of the battalion.   Though small groups totalling 150 men rejoined the battalion at a later stage in the campaign the three missing companies were never recovered.   Some who survived the action and dispersed to make their escape as best they could, were to die later in the jungle. John and his comrade Capt. Hart managed to effect an escape in a small boat, and after great hardship, to reach Sumatra.

In March 1990, my wife and I visited Kranji War Cemetery, just south of the Causeway linking Singapore to the mainland of Malaysia.   Occupying a small hilltop in a surprisingly rural location, remote from the hustle and bustle of the city, it was an impressively beautiful haven of peace and tranquility, kept in immaculate order.   On the top of the hill stood the Memorial itself with the grave spaces flowing down the gentle slopes to the perimeter wall and there in the central passageways, on no less than ten separate panels, each of them containing some forty two names, were recorded the names of the officers and men of our 2nd Battalion who had made the ultimate sacrifice.   The Memorial is an extensive building and though I did not carefully examine the whole of it, I made a cursory inspection without locating any other group of panels which might have demonstrated that any other battalion had paid anything like such a bitter price. We had come by taxi and were quite alone apart from the taxi driver who waited in the car park. We were not hassled by any other fellow travellers who wanted to be off; there was time to think, to remember and to give thanks.

After the War, John had even more extraordinary experiences, which are related in a book entitled "Strange Vagabond of God" by Father John Dove, S.J., who also served with the regiment during the War. John Bradburne proved to be a quite exceptional man. He came from a cultured background, but turned his back on what many might have regarded as "the good life" to become a monk - I think a Franciscan - and eventually ended up in a leper colony at a place called Mtemwa, not far from the city then known as Salisbury in Rhodesia (now Zimbabwe). There for some nine years, he lived with the lepers in a saintly life of total self-denial, sharing every aspect of their life, tending their wounds, nursing them through their sickness, burying them when they died, comforting them in their distress, teaching them and generally doing all he could to help them.

Towards the end of this period, there came the struggle for independence, with marauding bands of guerrillas roaming the countryside, wreaking vengeance on Europeans generally, without questioning whether they had or were doing anything for the good of the native community. In the early hours of 3rd September 1979 the guerrillas raided the Mtemwa Leper Camp and abducted John from his hut. On the 5th September his body, dressed only in his underpants, was found by the side of the main Mtoko-Nyamapanda road. He was lying on his back, his eyes were open and his right hand was under his head, with his left hand lying by his side. He had been shot repeatedly in the lower part of his back and in the legs, with an AK rifle and 24 spent cartridge cases were found at the scene. A witness later said that he had died like a "hwaiyana" (lamb), silent, without complaint.

If any man had ever lived as a saint during all those years, it was John, and there was just no rhyme or reason whatsoever in his killing. The funeral service took place five days later, at 10 am on the 10th September, at the local Catholic Cathedral, the body having been kept meanwhile in cold storage. Towards the end of the service, three white lilies were placed on top of the coffin, as it stood on trestles at the front of the Cathedral, and at that time three drops of fresh blood were seen to fall from the bottom of the coffin on to the floor.

At the conclusion of the service the coffin was removed to the funeral parlour and opened up. The body was found to be in a perfect state of preservation. The wounds were examined and found to be dry, there was no seepage and there was no blood or dampness within the coffin and a most careful examination left everyone mystified and without any explanation for the three drops of fresh blood. The opportunity was taken to fulfil John's wish - that he should be buried in the Franciscan habit - and the robe, not previously available, was provided for this purpose. There was overwhelming evidence that something quite sensational had occurred, and almost overnight John became world news. Judith, the Countess Listowel, a good friend of John and his brother Philip, spoke of him on the BBC.

How does one measure greatness of the human spirit?. This simple chronicle contains a number of instances where true human greatness shines like a shaft of sunlight to pierce the pervading gloom and horror of the battlefield. Within a space of time ranging, usually, from a few seconds to a few hours, a man or a group of men, lay aside all self interest and any thought of self preservation and , in an act of supreme gallantry, risk or lay down life itself for the benefit of their comrades. "Greater love hath no man than this, that a man lay down his life for his friends." John's life and death were an illustration of greatness of the human spirit on an entirely different plane. Not just for seconds or hours, but for year after year, for nine years in all until death intervened, he laid aside all thought of self interest and gave not just all that he had, but all that he was, without any reservation whatsoever, for the benefit of those needy lepers, whose physical condition most of us who have found repugnant in the extreme. Although I'm sure he did not think of it in this way, it was a display of enduring greatness of the human spirit, which it would be difficult to parallel. All those long years ago, at the mortar position below Point 2171, and elsewhere, we had rubbed shoulders with incipient human greatness of this supreme quality - and were quite unaware.

THE CLOSING STAGES.

It appeared from captured enemy documents that they had formed a special "Butai" or force to recapture Point 2171, and no doubt this was why we were receiving such careful and assiduous attention. In point of fact, this worked to our advantage rather than the reverse. Our own brigade position was most insecure, since we had been so weakened by heavy casualties and were so spread out on the ground that we had no brigade reserves at all. Had the enemy put in an attack behind us, so as to come in between Point 2171 and brigade around the clearing at the bottom of the hill, we could have been in a most awkward position, since we had no forces to put into the field against them. By continuing to attack us on Point 2171, they were giving us an opportunity to inflict casualties on them, without having to go out and search for them.

Meanwhile, Reggie Twelvetrees with "A" company, having been relieved at Lakhren by the arrival of the survivors of the Cameronians, came up the trail towards Point 2171, picking up the Kings Own from Padigataung and leaving that place secure in the hands of the West Africans. At Hkamutyang, just a couple of miles due north of Point 2171, they bumped stiff opposition and their leading platoon was encircled by the enemy. The Kings Own were too far behind them down the trail to be able to give any help, but the position was restored by a prompt counter-attack led by Subedar Yem Bahadur, who was awarded the Military Cross, mainly for this action, though sadly, Jemedar Sher Bahadur was killed. Reggie withdrew back down the trail, and a few days later made another attempt to get forward, but again met opposition and it was judged better that he should stay there, so that the threat of his presence might discourage the enemy from attacking the rather insecure rear of our brigade position. On the 13th July, Jacko took out a strong fighting patrol from "D" company and attacked the rear of the enemy position at Hkamutyang inflicting some casualties and also capturing a dump of 75 mm shells.

We were now right at the end of our period of active service. The order was given for us to withdraw, and on the afternoon of the 18th July, we moved out, without being molested in any way. The battalion now acted as advance guard, whilst 80 column took on the task of rear guard. The enemy were still on the tracks behind us, and so we made our way across country which involved cutting a pathway through dense bamboo thickets for much of our journey. This, and the fact that we were carrying about 100 casualties with us, cut down our progress to only four miles a day. On the 19th July we met up with The Black Watch from 14 Brigade, who were on their way to relieve us, incidentally exchanging a few harmless shots with them. In the jungle, their leading scouts mistook our men, with their Mongoloid appearance and small stature, as Japanese, but no harm was done. On 21st July we reached Hkum Pahok where we picked up "A" company and The King's Own.

Stilwell was continuing to insist that The Chindits should stay on, although Lentaigne argued that they had reached the end of their tether. At last a compromise was reached, the men of 77 and 111 Brigade would be medically examined, and those found to be unfit for further service should be evacuated, and the rest should stay on. This was not exactly a happy situation, because it amounted to a suggestion that The Chindits, despite all that they had done, were malingering. The medical examinations established that out of a total of 2,200 men only 118 men comprising seven British officers, twenty one British other ranks and ninety Gurkhas were fit for action. I suspect that even that frightening result - 95% unfit and only 5% fit, was over optimistic, because I was one of the British officers passed as fit, and yet when I got to India, I ended up in hospital for five weeks, with a fever which would not respond to treatment, and which, so far as I know, was never diagnosed, though I believe that tests established that my leucocyte (white cell) blood count was very low. I am sure it was a comfort to all of us to have Stilwell proved wrong, and to have it established after all that we were not malingering!.

We marched to Mla, and the wounded were taken to the excellent American hospital at Pahok, on the road almost due west of Mogaung, whence they were flown out by light planes using the road as a landing strip. We stayed at Mla for some days, and then marched along the road to Mogaung. After being for so many months confined to difficult jungle trails, it was restful to march on a road. On that road, we passed the British 36th Division, marching down the road in the opposite direction to take over where we'd left off. I remember that we were on a bank on the left hand side of the road, so they passed us on our right and at a lower level than us, so we had a good view of them all. Quite close to the front of their column, was the tall imposing figure of their general, Major General-Francis Festing, who was marching with his men. They all looked almost unbelievably fit and smart and carried themselves with a splendid military bearing, just like the real soldiers they were. By contrast, we looked pretty awful. We were gaunt and haggard, our uniforms hung loosely on our skinny frames, and we'd almost forgotten what a military bearing looked like! But perhaps, after all, we could claim to have acquitted ourselves like soldiers.

After a few days at Mogaung, we went by a jeep drawn train the 45 miles to Myitkyina, where the airport was operating and from there by Dakota to Tinsukia on the Bengal-Assam Railway. From Tinsukia, Alec and I flew on to Dehra Dun to make arrangements for the reception of the battalion, who came on by rail from Tinsukia with Reggie Twelvetrees. When the train drew into Dehra Dun station shortly before midnight on the 8th August the band of the Cameronians and also the regimental pipe band were there to greet the battalion, and ladies of the Women's

Volunteer Service served refreshments to all ranks before they embussed for our Regimental Centre at Birpur.

So ended a campaign which tested all of us to the limits of our physical endurance and beyond, and also made calls upon us as soldiers for acts of devotion and self-sacrifice above and beyond the call of duty. With all due humility, I think we can say that, as a battalion, we passed that test with flying colours, and that, as we look back over the years, each of us has every justification in saying with pride - "I was there!"

My story must end now. I have no more time, and this account must be despatched out to the battalion in India, and I hope they will find it of some interest and that it might help them in understanding a little more of what happened in our sector of the campaign. The script started out as being aimed at use by the battalion only, but as I progressed I decided to expand it so that it might be of interest to my family and some of my friends and perhaps some of the members of our regimental association here in the U.K. If some of the digressions are considered too long or irrelevant, perhaps my old battalion will just select the passages they need and discard the rest. I should like to have been able to say more about other units in The Chindits, particularly our own 4th battalion, who did wonders in Morrisforce, but I have had no secretarial help at all and have found the typing hard going.

FOOTNOTE.

Comments from those who have seen the typescript have encouraged me to have this account printed privately and I have taken the opportunity of making a few alterations and adding a few vignettes, but in substance the chronicle is as first prepared.

SOURCES

Personal Notes from Lt.Col. A.F.Harper, D.S.O.

"The 9th Gurkha Rifles Regimental History (Vol.2)" by Lt.Col. G.R.Stevens (1958)

"The Campaign in Burma" - HMSO 1946

"Wings of the Phoenix - The Official Story of the Air War in Burma" - HMSO 1949

"Burma - The Longest War 1941-45" by Louis Allen. Pub. 1984 by J.M.Dent & Sons, Ltd.

"The Chindit War - The Campaign in Burma 1944" by Brig. Shelford Bidwell. Pub. 1979 by Hodder and Stoughton.

"Chindit" by Rhodes James. Pub. 1980 by John Murray, Ltd.

"The Wild Green Earth" by Bernard Fergusson. Pub. 1952 by Collins.

Miscellaneous Papers at the Library of the Imperial War Museum.

Note: The finest account of the exploits of 77 Brigade is "Prisoners of Hope" by Brig. Michael Calvert, D.S.O., pub. Cape, London 1952.   "The Road past Mandalay" by Lt.Col. John Masters, D.S.O. pub. Michael Joseph, London 1961 contains a fine account of the activities of 111 Brigade. Sadly my copies of each of these books have gone "AWOL" and I was not able to refer to them.